Prepare the Way
with
POSTERS

Prepare the Way with POSTERS

Creative Poster-making to Attract and Inspire

Written and illustrated by

Yvonne Coppock

Cartoons by
Elizabeth Luxton

Photographs by
Richard Dorey

Gazelle
BOOKS

First published 1999 by Gazelle Books, Concorde House, Grenville Place, Mill Hill,
London NW7 3SA

ISBN 1 899746 18 8

ACKNOWLEDGEMENTS
Scripture quotations taken from the
Holy Bible, New International Version.
Copyright © 1973, 1978, 1984 by International Bible Society.
Used by permission of Hodder and Stoughton Ltd.

Permission has been kindly given by the poster-makers listed on page 6 to use
photographs of their posters. However, we have been unable to trace the person
who made "Alive not dead", featured on the front cover. If you recognise the poster
as yours, please contact the author.

Page 13 Photograph of gable-end poster hoarding, copyright Kirklees Metropolitan
Council, Huddersfield, reproduced by permission.

Page 38   Line drawing based on 'Skegness is so bracing', copyright Science
Museum, London, used by permission.

Page 38   Quotation from Worship by Graham Kendrick, copyright 1984, used by
permission of Kingsway Publications Ltd.

Page 13 of colour section. Poster based on harvest invitation design by CPO,
Worthing, used by permission.

Designed and produced for the publishers by Gazelle Creative Productions Ltd,
Concorde House, Grenville Place, Mill Hill, London NW7 3SA

A word about this book

You may have already flicked through this book looking at the pictures, and now be wondering whether you have time to sit down and read it properly.

Perhaps you feel happier making things than reading. You are keen to start making a poster straight away, and inclined to put the book on one side until later.

If that sounds like you, look at the *Contents* page, especially *Part Two,* which is the practical part. If one chapter interests you, read that one first and then keep the book handy, so you can refer to other chapters when you need more information.

You may, on the other hand, be someone who is unconvinced about the usefulness of posters or who thinks it safer to use ready-printed ones. *Part One* is for you. I hope, once you have read it, you will want to read *Part Two* as well, and even start making posters yourself.

I pray that everyone who opens this book will discover something in it that is either useful or fun, and that many will find fresh inspiration for poster-making in their own church.

Thanks

- to the Fisherfolk, for challenging the church to think in new ways

- to Nigel and Anne Holmes, who started us making posters at St Paul's

- to Priscilla Nunnerley, for encouraging me to believe this book was possible

- to the many Christian friends who have prayed and patiently supported me through the ups and downs of writing the book

- especially to Diana Archer, Hilary Brand, Wendy Maguire, Pam Le Clercq, Heather Brooks and Gerry Martin, for their contributions, comments and suggestions

- to my long-suffering family

- to Jill Moody, Lois Hesford, Eric Shand, Gary Vibert, Geraldine Maguire, Natalie Coppock, Clive Golding, Sharon John, Annette O'Connell, Kay Pollard, Barbara Hopkins, James Vasselin, Elizabeth Luxton, Annie Pope, Wendy Maguire, Eileen Agnes, Ray Middleton, Vivienne Dorey and Joy Wimberley, whose posters are featured in this book

- and to all the people over the years, who have shared the fun of poster-making and the thrill of seeing our posters used by God.

A SECOND BOOK – CAN YOU HELP?

This book is based largely on the experience of one church, St Paul's in Jersey.

A second book is planned, which will draw together ideas from many churches, to show the variety that is possible in poster-making, as well as organisation and display.

If your church makes posters, or you know of one that does, please write to:

Yvonne Coppock
7 Belvedere Drive
Belvedere Hill
St Saviour
JERSEY JE2 7RN.

WORKSHOPS

Yvonne Coppock is available to lead workshops at churches that would like to make posters but are not sure how to start.

Please contact her at the address above.

Contents

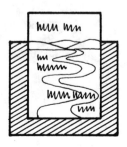

Prepare the Way

'... a voice of one calling in the desert,
  "Prepare the way for the Lord,
  make straight paths for him"'... (Luke 3:4)

We live in a confused and hurting world, where people
wander in a spiritual wilderness because they have forgotten how to listen to God.

A poster outside the church can be a voice in the desert, calling people to look up
from their everyday preoccupations – calling them to make way for the Lord who can
transform their lives.

Poster-makers have a key role in preparing the way for
those who do not normally come inside the church. Many
walk past without even noticing that the church is there. The
poster can attract attention and create interest without
exerting pressure.

Some posters act as simple sign-posts. Others offer
refreshment to weary travellers. Sometimes it may be right to
warn of danger ahead, like John the Baptist proclaiming,
'Repent, for the kingdom of heaven is near.'

Poster-makers may need to prepare the way inside the
church too. In most churches, music and flower-arranging are taken for granted, and
the paths of banner-making and drama are comparatively well-trodden. But poster-
making, if it happens at all, tends to be the domain of a solitary 'expert' or of children
in the Sunday School. I believe that there are many in our churches with the talents
required to make inspiring posters, but what has been lacking is leadership, coordination and the marshalling of resources.

It is easy to follow where others have been before but is God, perhaps, calling you
to strike out on a new path, to prepare the way so that others
can follow?

'... The crooked roads shall become straight,
  the rough ways smooth.
  And all mankind will see God's salvation.' (Luke 3:5&6)

PART ONE
WHY?

1 What is a poster?

Before considering why posters are needed, we need to think what the word **POSTER** means. What exactly is a poster and what makes it different from a **NOTICE** or a **BANNER**?

A **POSTER** is a **large** sheet of **paper** or **card**, 'posted' (ie stuck or pinned) in a **public** place to **advertise** something.

The look should be **simple** and the effect **immediate**. **Picture and words** together create a visual shorthand, so the poster can **attract attention** and **transmit its message** within a few seconds.

It has a **short life span** – its impact depends on **freshness** rather than on lasting beauty.

The aim is to **attract**, to **interest** and to **inform**, in that order.

A **NOTICE** is similar to a poster but uses words only, without the pictorial element. It provides information for people who already have reason to seek it, whereas a poster aims to attract those who would otherwise pass by.

A **BANNER** is normally made of fabric rather than paper and hangs, instead of being pinned or pasted. In the past banners were used, particularly in time of battle, to identify and draw together those committed to a common cause. In recent years, church banner-making groups have helped to revitalise worship and encourage commitment, and have shown how much artistic talent was lying dormant.

Posters have a different role. Using the language of everyday life and images people can relate to, they make God's Word accessible to those outside the church. This is one way of reaching people where they are, touching lives without causing embarrassment.

2 Why posters?

The need for publicity

If every church activity was well-advertised, the public would not assume, as it often does, that the church is dying. Often the problem is not lack of action but poor publicity. Special services are organised, flowers arranged and banners hung, videos are shown, visiting speakers come and go, exhibitions are set up, music and drama flourish... but people passing by have no idea that these things are happening.

There are basically two types of Christian poster: publicity posters that tell what we are doing and message posters that tell what we believe. Both are needed to show that God's church is alive and relevant.

Message posters and publicity posters.

A visual age

The arts need to have a place in the life of the church. By touching people's emotions and awakening the imagination, they heighten awareness of things that are usually taken for granted.

Why is it that music is accepted as a normal part of worship, while visual art is often viewed with suspicion? Perhaps there is a fear of the picture becoming an object of worship, instead of leading people to God.

If you want biblical justification for the visual arts, look at *Exodus 26:1-6* and *31:1-5*. Would God have given such detailed instructions for the building and decoration of the tabernacle if he had not wanted men and women to create beautiful things as an expression of their love for him?

Jesus did not carry felt pens and sheets of paper but he used words to paint vivid pictures in people's minds. The art form that was suited to his itinerant ministry and to the slow-moving culture of the time was storytelling. In first-century Palestine few people could read or write, so news, entertainment, education and information were all passed on by word of mouth. Jesus worked within that tradition and used the medium that was appropriate for his audience.

We learn through pictures.

But we live in a fast-paced and highly visual age. From earliest childhood we learn visually, first through pictures and later by means of the written word. We remember more easily what we have seen than what we have heard. In a world geared to thirty-second TV commercials, posters may accomplish more than sermons.

Posters can enrich dull lives

The posters that are so familiar on the platforms of the London Underground offer not only information but also interest and amusement for jaded commuters. Poster art is not intended to be shut away in art galleries, to be appreciated only by connoisseurs. It is part of everyday life – art of the people and for the people.

A few years ago I remember reading about two polar bears in a zoo who used to spend long hours pacing restlessly up and down, until a psychologist had the idea of providing an 'enrichment programme'. Toys such as traffic cones, plastic barrels and balls were introduced and food was presented in blocks of ice or scattered about the enclosure so that the bears had to search for it.

Why can't Christians introduce an enrichment programme of posters to bring interest and purpose into the lives of people who feel trapped and bored? With Jesus there is more to life than a weary pacing back and forth between home and work.

Visual parables

God created human beings – and polar bears – with a natural curiosity and desire to find things out for themselves. Making a discovery is more exciting than being told. (How much do you remember of last week's sermon…?) A personal discovery is more likely to stay fixed in the memory and more likely to lead on to positive action.

Jesus understood human psychology. His parables aroused interest but sometimes left the audience to puzzle out the meaning. The story of the farmer sowing seed (in *Luke 8*) was told to a large crowd, but Jesus did not give any explanation except to a small group of disciples when they asked him about it later. Parables can take time to sink in.

Posters, like parables, should provoke questions rather than give glib answers. A good poster will stimulate curiosity and invite an active response. People need to search and find God for themselves. They cannot be cajoled or bullied into the Kingdom.

God has prepared a banquet.

An invitation

God has prepared a banquet and tells us to go out into the city streets and into the country lanes and *'compel people to come in' (Luke 14:23 RSV)*. The advantage of doing this through posters is that a 'compelling' poster can persuade, while still allowing the person freedom of choice – freedom to look at the poster or ignore it, to respond to or reject the message. Our job is to make the invitation hard to resist!

Paul wrote (in *Romans 15:20*) of his *'ambition to preach the gospel where Christ was not known'*. Posters can reach out into that unclaimed territory without making people feel threatened.

A golden age for Christian posters?

One hundred years ago, Toulouse-Lautrec was designing posters in Paris, at the height of what has become known as the 'golden age' of posters. The new art-form soon caught the imagination of the public in other cities of Europe and North America. Posters jostled for position on crowded hoardings and were avidly collected.

In Britain, many of the best posters over the years have been produced for railway companies and, in particular, the London Underground. It seems likely that the abundance of display areas at stations and on trains played a major part in this development, since the cost of any poster campaign is greatly reduced if display facilities are owned by the advertiser.

There is a lesson here for the church. Church buildings exist in every town and village in the country, many strategically placed

Posters jostled for position on gable-ends of houses.

for maximum visibility. Not only does the church own more display areas than any other body of people who share a common aim, but it also has, sitting in its pews, potential artists to make the posters.

Perhaps we should be praying for a renaissance of poster art but with a new purpose – advertising not a holiday destination but an eternal one, not selling a product but introducing Jesus. If the church can learn to make use of its valuable resources, this may provide the impetus for a second golden age, this time of Christian posters.

3 Why make your own?

Why bother to make your own when you can buy posters designed by professional artists? Buying a few posters is in fact a very good way to start. As you learn how to display them to best advantage, you can assess which are most effective and most appropriate for your church.

However, posters need to be regularly changed, and ready-printed ones cost money. Also, you will discover that the supply of suitable posters is limited. As you gain confidence in your own judgement, you will find yourself thinking, 'If I had made that, I would have done it differently…' At that stage, you may want to try your hand at making some of your own. These can then be interspersed with bought posters, to achieve maximum variety and interest.

If you have a computer, you may think that its sophisticated design capabilities will solve all your problems. But it has limitations, the main one being the size of paper that you can feed into the printer. Sadly, an A4 poster will not make much impact on an outdoor notice-board.

Surprisingly, handmade posters often attract more attention than printed ones. Our eyes are so attuned to the regularity of the printed word, that anything different easily catches a passing glance. This is not an excuse for hastily scribbled messages. But handmade posters that are fresh and original have a distinct advantage over printed ones.

Economy

Making your own is certainly cheaper than buying, even from firms that print huge numbers to keep the prices low. If you ask a sign-writer to make posters to your specifications, or have them printed locally in small numbers, the price rises dramatically.

There is no cheaper form of publicity than making your own posters apart from passing on information by word of mouth, or making the church event so newsworthy that it gets free media coverage. (The ideal solution is to use all three methods!)

In a world of dwindling forests, economy of paper should also be considered. One poster seen by hundreds of people can be a sensible alternative to hundreds of leaflets, which may be quickly consigned to the litter bin.

Suitability for the location

Mass-produced posters are designed for a wide range of situations but may not be precisely what is needed in one particular place at a specific time. Handmade posters can be made to fit the requirements exactly.

Getting the size right is the first priority. Too small a poster will not be noticed. Too large a poster may be spoiled if it has to be trimmed to fit the notice-board. The size of the writing is also important – it needs to be suited to the viewing distance. Many of the widely-available Christian posters, which have words superimposed on a colour photograph, are more suitable for the walls of a living room than the display-board outside a church, because of the small size of the writing.

Handmade posters can give people an idea of what style of worship to expect. For instance, a youth event might call for a jazzy modern poster, while a traditional service needs a more formal approach.

Another benefit of making the posters yourself is that you can choose subjects of topical or local interest that passers-by can identify with.

Getting the size right.

The joy of creating

Poster-making is enjoyable, and all the more satisfying because it is useful as well as fun. With a little help, simple posters can be made by any member of the church – man or woman, teenager or child.

The desire to create is part of being made in the image of a creative God. Give a group of small children paints, brushes, crayons, glue and coloured paper and they

Creativity is unpredictable.

will have a wonderful time making pictures. They are not self-conscious or worried about what people will think. They simply enjoy the process of making something.

Why is it that so many adults believe they are not creative? What happened to that spontaneity we had as children? Our educational system is partly to blame, with its emphasis on the development of reason and logic, at the expense of emotion and intuition. But also, the drive to succeed in a competitive society can squeeze out the willingness to experiment and take risks.

Creativity is unpredictable – you don't know exactly how things will turn out. But Jesus said, *'Unless you change and become like little children, you will never enter the kingdom of heaven' (Matthew 18:13)*. Part of being childlike is being willing to return to the trustful risk-taking of childhood.

Being creative does not just mean being good at drawing or painting. You can be creative with a saucepan or a cricket bat, in office management or bringing up a family. It involves taking certain raw materials and working with them to produce something new. Our efforts at poster-making may seem rather feeble, like kneading a lump of heavy dough. But just as the heat of the oven changes dough into bread, so the fire of the Holy Spirit can transform our posters and use them to stimulate a healthy appetite for the *'true bread from heaven…who…gives life to the world' (John 6:32,33)*. If posters are fresh (not re-using yesterday's stale ideas), the aroma of Christ can waft out into the street, like the smell of freshly-baked bread from a hot bread shop.

Developing our talents

In many churches there is an untapped pool of creative energy waiting to be channelled into something worthwhile. I do not mean the recognised artists, whose talents are probably already being used, but the housewife at home all day with small children, the unemployed school-leaver with time on his hands, and those trapped in jobs that leave them feeling restless and dissatisfied. These people often have undiscovered talents, that need to be directed and encouraged. If you have a Bible handy, look at Jesus' parable of the talents in *Matthew 25*. There are several points worth noting:

1   The master entrusted *'his property'* to his servants *(verse 14)*. Whatever talents we may have, individually or as a church, they are God's property loaned to us on the understanding that we will use them in his service.

2   The man who received five talents went *'at once...'* *(verse 16)*. He did not waste time debating whether his master really wanted him to use his talents.

3   As we put our talents to work, they increase in value *(verse 16)*.

4   If your talent seems small compared with someone else's, you may be tempted to bury it *(verse 18)*.

5   The reward for faithful service is not idleness but more responsibility, as well as increased satisfaction *(verses 21 & 23)*.

You may be tempted to bury it.

6   The master was just as pleased with the man who made four talents out of two as with the man who made ten out of five *(verses 21 & 23)*. What is important in God's eyes is not how much talent we have, but how well we make use of it.

7   The third man says: *'I was afraid' (verse 25)*. Fear often holds us back – doing nothing seems safer than the risk of failure.

8   What did Jesus mean by putting the money on deposit at the bank (in *verse 27*)? Perhaps for us it means putting our talents at the disposal of the church. Combined with those of other people, they can be invested in projects which would be too big for one person to tackle alone. The important thing is to make sure our talents do not lie dormant when God wants them to be used.

The human touch

An empty notice-board implies that the church does not much care about those outside. Printed posters show that at least someone was interested enough to pin them up. But handmade posters give a friendly look, as if the church wants to make contact with the person walking past. They show the human face of the church, allowing some of its warmth, and perhaps its vulnerability, to spill out into the street.

Some time ago I walked into the fellowship area of our church and noticed a

Handmade posters show the human face of the church.

yoghurt pot stuffed full of wild flowers. I don't know who put them there or why, but that spontaneous gesture touched me in a way that the formal flower arrangements had never done. I cannot explain my reaction but I have discovered that posters sometimes work in a similar way. The message of a poster that is fresh and simple can go straight to the heart.

Poster-making can be described as 'back-door evangelism'. The informality of a handmade poster is like a relaxed conversation with a neighbour at the back door or over the garden fence, rather than a formal front-door visit from the vicar. Like a series of friendly chats, posters can build confidence and arouse interest over a period of time until the truth of the gospel strikes home.

'Power made perfect in weakness' (2 Corinthians 12:9)

Don't worry if you feel totally inadequate to the task of poster-making, or if you look at those alongside you and question whether they can ever be much use. If God seems to be nudging you in this direction, then trust him for the outcome.

We can sometimes be too concerned about methods and techniques. Our availability is more important to God than our ability. Under his guidance, we will learn better and more effective ways of getting the message across. But if we are hoping to perfect our technique before starting to make posters, there is little likelihood of ever starting at all. The aim is not to show people how clever we are but to point them towards God.

4 Why a group?

It may seem that the perfect solution to the problem of the empty notice-board is to appoint an 'expert', probably a trained artist, to take responsibility for making and putting up the posters.

Unfortunately, it is not as simple as that. The expert starts with great confidence and receives much praise. Others in the church, although they would like to make posters, feel inhibited by their less obvious skills, and leave him or her to do the job alone. But poster-making is more time-consuming than most people realise and without encouragement and a steady flow of fresh ideas, enthusiasm is hard to sustain.

The Body of Christ

Human beings were designed to work together and complement one another. God planned the church as a model of this. So why do we find it so difficult to share responsibilities and resources? Often we make excuses, based on insecurity, pride or laziness:

> 'It's easier to do the job myself than explain it to someone else...'
> 'He does it so well – I mustn't interfere...'

Instead of sharing the load and encouraging one another, one person struggles alone, while others feel left out because they have not been asked to help.

In *1 Corinthians 12:27*, Paul says: *'You are the body of Christ, and each one of you is a part of it.'* When we accept Jesus as Lord we automatically become part of his

Designed for co-operation and mutual support.

body and we need to discover what our function should be. One duty of the stronger members of the body is to enable weaker members to utilise their gifts. Helping someone else to make a poster may be harder and, initially, more time-consuming than making one yourself. It requires patience and commitment to mix paint or hold a stencil for a disabled friend, when you would prefer to be making your own poster. But from God's perspective, which is more worthwhile? *'Whatever you did for… these…, you did for me' (Matthew 25:40)*.

Learning to work as a team requires some effort, but the benefits far outweigh the difficulties. The people in your group may not be the ones you would have chosen, but you will be surprised how God can use the situation, if you let him. A common aim and shared enthusiasm make the process easier, and gradually a bond will be established, which is deeper than ordinary friendship.

Learning from one another

Outside the window of the room where I am writing grows a hawthorn tree, its bark wrinkled with age. One day as I was gazing out of the window, searching for some elusive word, I became aware of a little mouse-like treecreeper, picking his way in a careful spiral up the trunk of the tree, methodically probing for insects until, reaching the top, he flew down to the base of the next tree and started all over again.

You may be a methodical poster-maker, careful and precise, dependable and accurate, not wanting to draw attention to yourself. Or you may be more like the kingfisher, with his dazzling plumage, who makes an occasional dramatic dive, emerging with a glittering prize. Both birds simply do what comes naturally to them. Don't measure yourself against someone else who has different gifts. Find where your talent lies and enjoy what you are good at. Practise and persevere. But remember that we are not limited, as birds are, to one way of doing things. We can learn from one another and adapt to different methods.

The methodical treecreeper.

Pooling our talents

Some people have a good eye for colour, others a gift with words. Some have lettering skills, or flair in creating pictures, or organisational ability. When our varied talents are brought together and offered to God, we begin to see the power of the Holy Spirit instead of just the cleverness of man.

One of the most exciting results of working together is the cross-fertilisation of ideas. Just as some apple and pear trees will not bear fruit unless another similar tree is planted nearby, so we limit our fruitfulness if we try to work in isolation. One person may have the germ of an idea, but need someone else's help to put it into practice. Sometimes ideas emerge unexpectedly out of times of prayer and discussion.

If we are willing to pool our talents and help each other to improve, we can achieve more together than as separate individuals. As we learn to trust one another, we can discuss ideas and methods and help each other to avoid mistakes. I don't recommend my experience, of finishing a difficult poster once after struggling alone for hours, only to be informed that I had made a spelling mistake!

A prayerful group also provides a safeguard against inappropriate messages being displayed outside the church. If poster-makers have already learnt to share ideas and pray together, it is easier to eliminate an unsuitable message before it reaches the drawing-board. Discussing ideas at an early stage can prevent the pain caused by rejection of a poster after it is finished.

Variety

God created a world full of diversity. Variety makes life interesting. Whether we are looking at wild flowers in the hedgerow, clothes in a shop window, vegetables in the market or scenery in a holiday brochure, variety brings stimulation and refreshment.

It is difficult for one person making posters alone to introduce enough variety to keep regular passers-by interested. A group, sharing its resources of experience and skill, ideas and materials, can be living proof of the abundant life that Jesus offers.

Unity, but not uniformity

It is not easy to achieve unity in a group, without tending towards uniformity. Uniformity may be imposed, with the best of intentions, by one person with a dominant personality. Or it may be the result of everyone trying to keep everyone else happy, putting up with second best rather than risking conflict. The aim, instead, should be that deeper unity which will bring out the best in each person – a relationship that allows freedom to be honest with one another.

Individuality, but not individualism

'Do not conform any longer to the pattern of this world, but be transformed by the renewing of your mind', says Paul in Romans 12:2.

There are three very different ways in which, without realising it, we may be tempted to conform:

1 **Tradition** – clinging to the security of doing things the way they have always been done.
2 **Fashion** – slavish adherence to whatever is the latest craze.
3 **Individualism** – succumbing to a climate where we are continually urged to 'do our own thing'.

Individualism.

I know from personal experience that a rebellious spirit can limit one's usefulness to God. Since my teens, I have always wanted to be different, not to be just one of the crowd. A few years ago, a visiting speaker at my church was talking about the unhelpful aspects of individualism and as we prayed afterwards I had a vivid picture in my mind of myself as a sheep in the middle of a flock of other woolly-backed sheep. At first, I did not much like the picture. But I knew that was where God wanted me to be.

Working in a team does not mean sacrificing our God-given individuality. Remember, Jesus knows each sheep by name. He understands better than anyone our individual characteristics, yet he knows how important it is for us to stay close to each other and to him. Within the security of a supportive group, we can develop our varied talents without the extremes of individualism.

Co-operation, not competition

It is all too easy to allow a competitive attitude to creep into church activities. Paul recognised this in his letter to the *Philippians (chapter 2, verses 3 and 4)*:

'Do nothing out of selfish ambition or vain conceit, but in humility consider others better than yourselves. Each of you should look not only to your own interests, but also to the interests of others.'

In making posters, there is a danger of being too concerned about what other people think. If we are not very self-confident we may feel the need to prove ourselves.

Be realistic about your weaknesses and your strengths, willing to receive help as well as give it. Encourage one another, especially in times of difficulty or disappointment. As you learn to work with others, Jesus will help you to let go of self-consciousness and pride, to be more truly the person he designed you to be.

The creative process is like a tender plant pushing up through the soil. It is easily crushed in the early stages and may need to be left to develop without interference. Don't be quick to offer advice until you have built up a relationship. Initially, all that is needed is feeding (provision of suitable materials), watering (encouragement) and space to develop without competition. Pruning and training can wait until roots are firmly established.

Feeding, watering and space to develop.

Once you know each other well, don't be too afraid of conflict – a certain amount of friction may be unavoidable in a group that is moving forward. If you never disagree, it may be that you have settled into a rut. Like-minded people will experience less conflict, but less stimulation or excitement. Friction can be creative or destructive, depending on the willingness of group members to work through momentary irritations. We need to ask God's help in dealing with the causes, rather than allowing minor differences to develop into long-term resentments. Sparks may fly, but striking sparks off one another can be God's way of generating new ideas.

Shared responsibility

Learning to co-operate as a group opens the way for growth and continuity. Where responsibility is shared and each person has a useful part to play, the work will continue even if the leader moves on. Ideally, leaders should be aiming to work themselves out of a job. Training others does not mean asking them to do the menial tasks, while the leader makes the creative decisions. Those who feel that their viewpoint is never given serious consideration will soon lose interest.

The job of leading a poster group might not involve making posters at all. The leader may just be a co-ordinator, organising meetings, buying materials and putting up posters made by other people. Gradually some or all of these jobs can be taken on by others.

The most important role for the leader is to be a catalyst, the person who makes things happen. Helping people to catch the vision, motivating them to get started and keeping the momentum going are the main requirements for fruitful ministry.

Encouragement is a job for all the group, not just the leader. *'Encourage one another and build each other up'*, said Paul in *1 Thessalonians 5:11*. The fragile confidence of a poster-maker can easily be shattered by a negative comment at the wrong moment. Remember that the person who talks big probably feels very small inside. A quiet ministry of encouragement can work wonders. **Be generous with praise and sparing with advice.**

STARTING A GROUP

What can you do if you seem to be the only person interested in poster-making in your church?

1 **Be willing to accept God's choice of partners.** The most common block to finding companions is our fear that God will ask us to work with someone we don't like. *'Lord, send me some poster-makers to work with, but please, not So-and-so…'* Who knows, perhaps even Jesus felt like that about some of his disciples! Bring your doubts and fears honestly to God. Once you are willing to follow God's plan, rather than your own, you may become aware of people you would never have considered suitable, but whom God has been preparing.
2 **Ask people individually.** People seldom volunteer for jobs in the church, but if asked whether they would like to be involved, they often say yes.
3 **Send out a letter to other churches** in your area, inviting anyone interested in making posters to a meeting. Even if only one person turns up, you have made a start. Plan to meet regularly and see how the Lord leads you.
4 **Keep praying!**

ORGANISING THE POSTER-MAKING

This is how the poster work has evolved at St Paul's Church in Jersey. Use our system as a model if you wish, but adapt it and develop your own method according to the needs of your congregation.

The Workshop

At St Paul's, a continuing supply of new posters is achieved through a flexible system of poster workshops, which are open to any Christian who has a desire to serve God in this way. We are fortunate in having the use of a former school building and a large walk-in cupboard in which to store materials and finished posters.

1 First, a **date and time** for a workshop are fixed to suit the needs of the people most likely to come.
2 An **open invitation** is issued, through the church's weekly news sheet and by word of mouth, to anyone in our church or from other churches who would like to try their hand at making posters. The number of people at a workshop might be anywhere between two and ten.

3 Since we are able to keep a good stock of materials permanently in the cupboard, little **advance preparation** is needed. If we are expecting several new people, we lay out a selection of interesting materials, and books relating to poster design, as well as displaying plenty of posters on the walls to stimulate ideas.

4 Our workshops always start with a time of **discussion** (about general aims or specific poster ideas) followed by **open prayer**. This can be difficult when people don't know each other or are not used to praying aloud, but it is important to be open to one another and aware of the presence of Jesus. As people begin to relax in each other's company they share more freely.

5 The first things the participants need are plenty of scrap paper, pencils and rubbers, so that they can start doodling and trying out ideas. Even if they know exactly what they intend to do, it is wise to do a **rough sketch** first to make sure the layout is pleasing to the eye.

6 If someone sits glumly looking at a blank sheet of paper, obviously devoid of ideas, we encourage them to **look around** at posters, at books (including the Bible and Christian song books) and at the materials that are available. Some people may have a glimmer of an idea without knowing quite how to put it into practice. Asking questions and **helping people to develop their own ideas** is better that telling them what to do.

7 When ready, each person will select a sheet of white, black or coloured **card for the background** and decide **what method** to use (paint, collage, pens, pastels...)

8 Then comes the exciting period, when **posters** actually begin to **take shape**, each one unique to the person making it.

9 A few people do not like the idea of making their posters in a workshop situation, preferring to work without distractions and without the feeling that others are

Each poster is unique to the person making it.

looking over their shoulder. We still encourage them to come along to discuss ideas, to pray and to see what others are doing. **Working quietly in an adjoining room** is a possible alternative to making posters alone at home.

10 The final stage of the workshop is important. Make sure the posters don't disappear into a cupboard, never again to emerge into daylight. If possible, they should be **pinned up immediately** so that they can be seen by all the participants before they go home. How the posters are used afterwards can be difficult to decide, but remember that people are easily discouraged and may be tempted to give up unless they feel their effort was appreciated.

11 **Two hours** seems to be about the right length for each workshop session, with perhaps a cup of tea or coffee in the middle. Less than one and a half hours does not allow much time for prayer and discussion, for ideas to develop and a start to be made on the actual poster. On the other hand, if a session is allowed to drag on too long, concentration is lost and enthusiasm wanes.

The Planning Group

Flexibility is desirable to enable people to develop their talents in a variety of ways, but efficient organisation is also important to avoid waste of time, energy and resources. A few years ago we became aware that the poster work at St Paul's needed to be better co-ordinated. A planning group of four members was established, meeting once a month,

- to decide which posters will be put up outside the church each week,
- to plan workshops and occasional exhibitions, and organise publicity for them,
- to keep the materials cupboard tidy and well-stocked and
- to pray together.

5 Why involve the church?

Before you start...

It is no good making posters to put up outside if you do not have the support of the rest of the congregation, and particularly the church leaders. If your church has never displayed posters and has no tradition of banners or visual aids, then don't expect changes to happen overnight. People need time to adjust to new ideas.

If those in authority are doubtful about the need for posters, the best way to start may be by offering to help publicise special services such as Christmas, Easter, Harvest and Mothering Sunday. Make sure the information is simple, clear and correct. Discuss what is required and what sort of picture and style would be appropriate, rather than making the poster in your own way without consultation. Ask your minister if he would like you to make posters to link with sermon themes or the church calendar. Support him in what he is doing and he is more likely to take an interest in what you would like to do.

If the door does not open at once, God may have other work for you to do in the meantime. Find other outlets for your skills. Are there existing posters or notices in the church which need rejuvenating or updating? (Check first with the person who made them.) Is help needed with visual aids for sermons or Sunday School? Are words or pictures needed for the overhead projector? Try your hand at designing bookmarks or greeting cards to give to your friends. Practise drawing, painting, lettering. If God has called you specifically to make posters, he will not keep you waiting for ever.

Don't expect changes to happen overnight.

Whatever happens, do not be tempted to rush ahead without the approval of your minister. In the meantime:

1 **Pray,** asking God to give you patience and the wisdom to know when the time is right.
2 **Know your aims.** Clarify what you hope to achieve through making posters.
3 **Decide how the posters will be displayed.** People are more likely to get excited about making posters if they know that their work will serve a specific purpose. Does your church have a suitable display board? Bear in mind that if posters get damaged by rain, enthusiasm will be dampened too.

The posters speak for the church

Many people never go inside a church. The only indication they have of what it stands for is what they see outside. An empty notice-board, or none at all, suggests 'Nothing much going on' or 'We're not interested in telling you what's going on'. Cheerful, friendly posters with a clear message are a sign of a welcoming church that knows what it believes.

But words need to be backed by action. A message about new life in Jesus will not ring true if the church building looks permanently neglected. If your poster says 'Welcome', make sure people will feel welcome when they come inside.

Equally, action needs publicity. It is a waste of time organising events that are poorly attended because no-one knows about them.

> **OUR AIMS AT ST. PAUL'S**
>
> **1** To attract, interest and inform those who do not know Jesus; to encourage and inspire those who do.
>
> **2** To discover and develop artistic talent lying dormant in the church.
>
> **3** To work together as a group, enjoying each other's company and learning from one another.

ASK FOR HELP

Once you have the go-ahead to start making posters, there are several ways in which other people can help:

Prayer

If you want other church members to pray for the poster work, they will need to feel involved with what you are doing. Feed them regularly with

Words need to be backed by action.

information about problems, successes and future plans. Be honest about your failures. If you never make mistakes, there may seem little point in praying. Don't expect everyone in the church to be totally committed to what you are doing. Most will have other priorities. However, interest will grow over a period of time.

Not everyone finds prayer easy. Some people will prefer to offer practical help.

Money

Ideally, the church should pay for necessary materials and equipment. Failing that, occasional money gifts from individuals will enable the poster-makers to get on with the job to which God has called them.

Materials

Many items can be found in the homes of church members. Circulate a list of needs: scrap paper for rough sketches, wallpaper, wrapping-paper, fabric, rulers, rubbers, pens and pencils, paint and brushes, old posters, magazines and calendars... Ask people to pass on any unwanted clutter that might be useful to you.

Skills

1 Someone with computer skills (and access to a computer) would be an enormous help for posters on which a lot of written information needs to be presented clearly.
2 Do you have a photographer in the congregation, who might like to be involved in the poster work?
3 Professional artists, architects and art teachers probably prefer to do something different in their spare time, but they might be willing to make an occasional poster or offer advice on materials and techniques.

4   If your church does not have its own photocopier, is there someone who would do photocopying for you?

Comments

If your aim is harmony within the church, be open to suggestions. People do not usually offer comments unless asked, but that does not mean that they have no opinion. In my own church, we have a poster exhibition from time to time, to give people a second chance to see the posters. A simple questionnaire encourages them to think why they like or dislike certain posters, and to suggest ways of improving. Most people are very restrained and polite in their comments, some are effusive in their praise, a few disarmingly frank, but it is always useful to have some idea of what their response has been.

A few are disarmingly frank.

Ideas

You may find that once you start making posters, the ideas come thick and fast. It is still good to ask members of your church to pass on any poster ideas they may have. If their ideas are used, these people will feel more involved in the work, and it may be that some of them can be encouraged to make posters themselves.

New poster-makers

Always leave the door open for new people to try their hand at poster-making. Encourage them to do something simple the first time, rather than embarking on a masterpiece that may become a spectacular failure! As they, and you, begin to discover their capabilities, they can extend their repertoire. Even if people only ever make one poster, they are more likely afterwards to take an interest in what other poster-makers are doing.

Handling Criticism

Criticism is hard to take, especially if it is directed against a poster you have made yourself. Most people are particularly vulnerable while actually making the poster and immediately afterwards. A few weeks later it is easier to be objective about it. Remember too that you are more likely to overreact if you are tired or under pressure.

If some church members, possibly the older ones, do not understand what you are doing, listen carefully to what they have to say. Explain your aims and intentions

A masterpiece that may become a spectacular failure.

and your reasons for putting up the poster in question. However frustrated you feel, make sure you have really understood the criticism, in order to be able to handle it appropriately. Don't jump to conclusions based on your own particular sensitivities.

Weigh up the seriousness of the criticism. Is it a casual remark or an important principle, a matter of personal taste or of fundamental doctrine? Is it the opinion of just one person or a more general attitude in the church? Pray about the problem, with the person concerned, or with someone else you can trust to be impartial and discreet. It may still be right to put up a poster, even when someone has expressed disapproval. If you have been given authority to choose which ones to display, you may have to make the final decision. If in doubt, consult your minister or other mature Christians before going ahead.

Remember that the posters outside the church are primarily aimed at non-Christians. The humorous poster that amuses and interests a young man on his way to the pub, and helps him to see that Christianity connects with real life, may seem flippant and irreverent to the elderly lady who has sat in the same pew in church for the last sixty years. Humour is a powerful tool but needs careful handling.

Encourage people who offer criticism to suggest a positive alternative. By applying their minds to the problem, they will begin to appreciate the difficulties involved. Someone interested enough to offer comments might become a future recruit to poster-making, or a prayer partner.

Build good relationships with the people doing other jobs in the church. Offering to make a poster to publicise the new children's playgroup or the youth club barbecue (making sure you co-ordinate closely with those involved and get the information correct) is one way of building bridges. We will not always agree on every detail of church life but we must maintain love and respect for one another.

'May the God who gives endurance and encouragement give you a spirit of unity...'
(Romans 15:5).

PART TWO
HOW?

6 The idea

If you are bursting with ideas, then skip this chapter. However, if your brain seems as blank as an empty sheet of paper, read on. Up to now, you have probably not been looking at the world with posters in mind. Ideas grow out of everyday life, but you need to train your mind to recognise the possibilities. The more posters you make, the more you will begin to see ideas in unexpected places.

An empty sheet of paper.

Ask God

If you want to make Christian posters, the first thing to do is to ask God to inspire you. The Creator of the universe is not short of ideas and he does not want to keep them all to himself. Too often we forget (or are too proud) to ask him.

Keep your eyes and ears open

God can pop a thought into your head without you expending any effort at all. But he wants partners, not robots. Since human beings need materials to create with, God provides the ingredients and encourages us to find ways of putting them together.

Ideas should come from your own experience. Keep a notebook and jot down (or sketch) little things that interest or amuse you. The aim is to show God's perspective on everyday matters.

Develop your imagination

Are you wary of the word imagination?... afraid that by allowing it free rein you might somehow lose your grip on reality? Like all God's gifts, the imagination can be used for good or allowed to run out of control. Look at Jesus' imaginative teaching methods – his use of parables and word-pictures, questions and puzzles to awaken interest and stimulate response. What a refreshing change after the fossilised legalism of the Pharisees. It is all too easy, whether preaching or teaching, making music or designing posters, to revert to the rule-book.

If your imagination is lying dormant, let God reactivate it. Like the body, it needs to be exercised and nourished if it is to grow. How about trying out a new recipe or rearranging your living room? Find a new route to work, or read a poem, or buy a ticket for the theatre. When you are out of doors, look at your surroundings with fresh eyes and think how you would describe them to someone who has never been there. Allow God to guide you into areas you have not yet explored and you will find ideas will begin to come bubbling to the surface.

SOURCES OF IDEAS

Illustrations in this book

Permission is given for any of the posters or illustrations in this book to be copied or adapted for church posters. If they are used for any other purpose, permission must first be obtained from the publisher (address on page 4). If possible, use the pictures as launch pads for your invention, rather than copying slavishly. Illustrations in other books are protected by copyright and should not be copied without permission.

The Bible

Let the Bible be your main source of inspiration. Hazy recollections of a few favourite passages are not enough. Read it regularly, preferably in a modern translation, asking God to speak to you through its pages. Keep a notebook with your Bible to record any words or images that might be suitable for a poster. But think carefully, before using them, whether the phrase that is meaningful to you will make sense to someone who has never read the Bible. See page 45 (The Message).

Read the Bible regularly.

Prayer

It is surprising how often we need God's help but forget to ask. Even if we do remember to ask him for poster ideas, we may miss the answer if we are too busy to listen.

Don't be content to pass on only what you have heard from other people. Learn to listen to God for yourself, as he speaks through the words of the Bible or plants thoughts in your mind as you pray. Establishing a habit of prayer is not easy. To understand what God is saying to you, make time to deepen your relationship with him. Note down those half-thoughts that are gone almost as soon as they have formed in your mind. Some ideas do not come fully-fledged but need time to develop and mature.

Jesus demonstrated the importance of spending time with God in the middle of a hectic schedule. In *Mark 1:35* we read: *'Very early in the morning, while it was still dark, Jesus got up, left the house and went off to a solitary place, where he prayed'.* If you think he wasn't as busy as you are, read the rest of the chapter!

The church

Church life

Take a notebook with you to church on Sunday. That telling phrase in the sermon will be difficult to recall once the preacher has moved on to his next point. You may also find poster ideas in hymns, choruses or prayers. If church services are planned ahead, posters can be linked with sermon titles or general themes. Make sure too that you keep informed about future outreach events, so that publicity posters can be discussed and planned well in advance. Nothing is more frustrating than having a brilliant idea when it is too late to put it into effect.

Other church members

Ask for ideas from other members of the church. Focus attention on posters a few times a year by organising a display or a series of workshops. Make it clear that you are open to suggestions from people other than those already involved in poster-making. Ask God to lead you to others whose gifts have not yet been identified, who may be too shy to say anything. An 'ideas box' in the church allows donors to remain anonymous if they wish. Or call it a 'swap shop', where people can give or take suggestions.

Discussion

Inspiration for posters may emerge from general discussion in housegroups, but a specific meeting exploring, sharing and trying out poster ideas is even better. Talking about your idea may not be easy. If it is still at embryo stage, you may be afraid of being laughed at. At the other extreme, a carefully worked-out concept can make us feel possessive, and reluctant to let anyone spoil it. But being willing to discuss openly enables us to reap the benefits of shared experience. A chance remark may set new trains of thought in motion. Half-formed ideas can be developed and refined. It must be agreed before you start, however, that each person is free to accept advice or reject it without giving offence.

The church building

Look around your church for ideas. Could the solid church tower be used to illustrate God's dependability? Or does the movement of the weathercock suggest the Christian's responsiveness to the wind of the Spirit? Perhaps the stonework reminds you of *1 Peter 2:5*

> '...*you also, like living stones, are being built...*'

Take a careful look at the pews and the kneelers, the pulpit and the font, the pattern of the organ-pipes and the shape of the windows. Does a poster idea lie

The solid church tower.

hidden in one of these? How about a drawing of the church door with a word of welcome, to encourage someone to take that first step across the threshold?

The beauty of nature

After a day spent sitting at a desk, a breath of fresh air and a glimpse of sky and trees refreshes the spirit, and reminds us that God is still there. In a similar way, a poster that recreates rugged cliffs or a flower-filled meadow can bring a moment of refreshment in a busy day. God's hand is at work, even in the city: delicate ferns grow out of a cracked wall, sparrows look for sandwich crumbs... If our eyes are open to God's little surprises, we can pass on our discoveries by reproducing them on paper.

The news

Read the newspaper as well as the Bible. If there is to be any real communication with those who pass by, the poster-maker must be in touch with what is going on in the world. The church sometimes appears to be more concerned with internal problems, such as the upkeep of church buildings, than with issues of world importance. People disturbed by TV images of drought in Africa or a motorway crash in Britain need to be reminded that with God nothing is impossible, that God is present in and can bring good out of every situation, however horrific. Posters can touch hearts but also encourage practical involvement through prayer and financial assistance.

Local events

Where possible, find links with local events and situations. Some ideas can be quite simple – for instance, *'Vote for Jesus'* at local election time, or (in Jersey) a poster with flowers on it during the week of the 'Battle of Flowers' festival.

Deeper issues, such as homelessness or unemployment, need to be treated with sensitivity. To someone without a bed for the night in the middle of winter, a poster saying *'God cares for the homeless'* might not be much comfort, if the church doors are locked and all the members have returned to their comfortable homes. Read the Bible prayerfully, alert for passages relevant to current problems. In the case of the homeless person, a picture of someone sleeping in a shop doorway with some sparrows in the foreground, and Jesus' words *'Don't be afraid; you are worth more than many sparrows' (Matthew 10:31)*, might be more appropriate.

If we use themes that are likely to connect with what is uppermost in people's minds, we can rely on God to provide the 'coincidence' of the right person passing at the right time.

The world of advertising

Train yourself to look with a critical eye at advertisements in newspapers and magazines, analysing why some work well and others are barely noticed. When you look at an advertising poster, ask the question 'Does it achieve its purpose?' How good is its use of colour, contrast, balance, simplicity, freshness (the five main elements of poster design)? Adapt other people's ideas or use them as jumping-off points. But remember that copying someone else's design is likely to be an infringement of copyright.

Keep a scrapbook

Cut out anything that interests you from magazines, food packets, bottle labels, carrier bags, greeting cards, wrapping paper and the junk mail that comes through your letter-box. You could divide the scrapbook into sections: lettering styles, logos, line drawings, photographs, colour schemes, layout.

Road-signs and pictorial symbols

Road-signs are designed for instant recognition even when passed at speed, and so they are an ideal model for the poster-maker. Other examples of instant communication are shop signs, 'logos' (ie what used to be called the trademark of a company) and pictorial symbols, used internationally to avoid language problems (the most common of which are the man and woman on the doors of public toilets). Dover's *Handbook of Pictorial Symbols* is an excellent source of copyright-free material.

Some pictorial symbols from the Dover handbook.

Can you think of a Bible verse to go with any of these?

The library

Browse through your local library, especially the design section. Don't despise the junior library – clear and well-illustrated children's books provide an easy way of mastering new skills, such as collage or potato printing. Keep an eye on your local bookshop too. If you can't afford to buy an expensive book, you may be able to persuade the library to order it.

The local school

If you are neither a teacher nor a parent of school-age children, find an opportunity to look around a school when they have an open day. The art department of a secondary school will be an eye-opener if your own experience of school art was formal and unadventurous.

Artwork produced by primary schools and even playgroups is also worth looking at because young children are wonderfully open-minded and unselfconscious. When you see the bright paintings produced by four and five-year-olds, you may be encouraged to have a go yourself. Whichever school you visit, notice the different techniques used and ask questions. Pupils and teachers will be pleased that someone is taking an interest in what they have done.

You will not like everything you see, but allow your preconceived ideas to be shaken about a bit!

Your notebook

I expect by now you've got the message: keep your notebook handy! Unless you write it down, the idea that flashes into your mind as you drive to work will be lost before the first coffee break. Words are harder to remember than pictures. Jot them down quickly before you get distracted because it is difficult to recapture the exact phrase later. The back of a shopping list will do, but a small notebook and pen in your pocket or handbag is a safer way of keeping your poster ideas together.

Start a poster collection

To begin with, collect any posters you can lay your hands on. You will become more selective as your taste develops.

Bookshops, travel agents, video and music centres are likely places to find advertising posters. If you see one you like, ask if you can have it when they take it down. Art galleries, museums and theatres often have posters for sale, as well as specialist poster shops. If you have students in the family, ask them to look out for interesting posters for you – college notice-boards are a fertile breeding ground for new ideas.

If you have nowhere to display your collection, or a family that does not share your taste, see if you can lay claim to one door in the house and invest in a packet of Blu-tack. Change the poster frequently and watch people's reactions.

The pressures of life

The most powerful posters sometimes emerge out of painful circumstances. Graham Kendrick, the Christian songwriter, says in his book *Worship*:

> *'Inspiration, in my experience, does not so much float out of a clear sky as get washed up on the beach in a storm!... It often takes an extreme of emotion or conviction to crystallize a particular truth and make it real enough to become the raw material for creativity'.*

Any door will do!

When you are going through a time of pressure or conflict, grief or depression, you may feel that you are not much use to God. But God can use these times to inspire in a special way. Remember Paul's words in *2 Corinthians 4:7*: *'We have this treasure in jars of clay to show that this all-surpassing power is from God and not from us.'*

Two examples spring to mind from my own church. One young woman, lying in a hospital bed after being told that she had cancer, saw a vision of Jesus standing firm and secure on a great rock, lashed by stormy seas. She was later able to make that picture into a poster. A second poster, of a lifeboat heading out to sea with the words *'Jesus saves'*, was made by a woman whose husband had recently been drowned at sea.

GOD'S INEXHAUSTIBLE SUPPLY

If you are feeling frustrated because you still have no inspiration, sit down quietly and ask yourself a few questions:

1 What are your motives for wanting to make posters? Be honest. Are you doing it to please God or anxious to make something that people will admire?
2 Are you afraid to commit yourself to an idea that may not be clever enough? The simplest are usually the best, so don't let fear hold you back.
3 Is there something else that God wants you to do first? Be patient. Perhaps your church is not yet ready for posters.
4 Does God want you to accept the discipline of working as part of a team? Receiving ideas through other Christians is a way of strengthening the Body, rather than fostering individual pride.

Whether your ideas come thick and fast, one at a time or very rarely, remember that the source is inexhaustible.

'How precious to me are your thoughts, O God!
How vast is the sum of them!
Were I to count them,
they would outnumber the grains of the sand.'
Psalm 139:17&18

If every church in the world had a new poster each week, God's supply of ideas would still never dry up. But we need to learn to listen to his voice.

7 The message

Once your imagination has been stimulated, you may have a profusion of ideas. But, for a successful poster, words and picture need to transmit a single idea. So this is the time to start thinning, weeding and pruning.

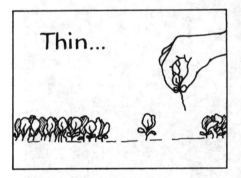

Thin to one idea for each poster

As with lettuce seedlings, avoid overcrowding. It is tempting to combine several related ideas in one poster, but by cramming in too much, you weaken the impact. If the ideas are too good to discard, separate them and make a series of posters. Give each seedling a chance to take root in people's minds without the competition of others.

Weed out negative ideas

Make your message positive. It is easy to slip into an anxious or a judgmental frame of mind and unconsciously pass this on through our posters. Instead, feed your mind on *'whatever is true.....* *lovely.....excellent.....praiseworthy'* *(Philippians 4:8)*. This does not mean closing our eyes to reality (posters must reflect the real world) but seeing things from God's perspective and enabling others to do the same.

Notice that truth comes first on that list in Philippians. Avoid exaggeration and half-truth, however well intentioned. Instead, with creativity, enthusiasm and humour show that 'good' does not mean 'dull'.

Prune unnecessary words

Cut the number of words to a minimum. The fewer there are, the more likely they are to be read. Unless the message is assimilated in a few seconds, the opportunity has probably been lost. By reducing the number of words, you also make your own job easier. Designing a poster with five words is fun. Organising a legible and interesting layout with twenty-five words is hard work.

A poster should be as economical with words as a telegram. Remember that the picture will play its part in conveying the meaning.

USING WORDS TO COMMUNICATE THE GOSPEL

The function of words is communication. But words can also mislead. We need to use them as accurately as possible and be aware that a word can mean different things in different situations. Can we find ways of bridging the gap between God's Word revealed in the Bible and the secular culture of the man or woman in the street? The job of the poster-maker is to make that link.

There are three aspects to this question which we will look at in turn: first **the context of the Bible**, second **the commission of the poster-maker** and third **the connection with the poster-viewer.**

I THE CONTEXT OF THE BIBLE

If you are using words from the Bible, make sure you have understood them and quoted them correctly. Read the whole passage – check the circumstances, who was writing (or speaking) and who the words were originally intended for. If the subject of your poster is not taken directly from the Bible, is it in tune with the teaching of the Bible? The picture should reinforce the real meaning of the words, not introduce a different idea. For example, if you were using the words *'Seek first his kingdom... and all these things will be given to you as well' (Matthew 6:33)*, a picture of luxury furniture, hi-fi equipment and a gleaming Porsche would be misleading. In the rest of this passage Jesus was talking about food, drink and clothes – our needs, not our wants.

Be selective but be careful

Is it permissible to leave out parts of a Bible verse? I believe there is scriptural justification for this. On several occasions, Jesus highlighted a few words that encapsulate an Old Testament truth rather than quoting the passage in full. See *Luke chapter 4, verses 4, 8 and 12* (quoted from *Deuteronomy 8:3, 6:13 and 6:16*). In *verses 18 and 19* of the same chapter of Luke, Jesus significantly left out *'the day of vengeance of our God'* when quoting *Isaiah 61:1 & 2*, presumably because he knew those words were not appropriate on that occasion.

But be careful. This does not give us a free hand to rewrite the Bible. There is always the danger that in leaving something out we may change the sense of what is being said. Be sure that you have understood the verse within its context. Does your poster convey the same meaning? Even a word for word quotation from the Bible does not guarantee correct interpretation, as we see in *Luke 4:10 and 11*. The devil can quote scripture too. God's Word has power to change lives but we need wisdom in the way we handle it.

Words can lose their freshness

Overused words become tired. Familiarity and repetition have eroded the shock factor from many of Jesus' sayings. (Bear in mind, though, that what is commonplace to us may be totally unexpected to someone who never goes to church.)

'This is my body. Take…eat…' does not send shock waves through a congregation about to take Communion. But imagine a poster showing Jesus' body marked off in sections like a carcass of beef. Our revulsion at that image gives us some idea of the reaction of the disciples when they first heard those words. Imagine eating the flesh of one's dearest friend! As to drinking blood, for a devout Jew that was unthinkable.

It is pointless making posters that offend without good reason. But shock tactics are sometimes necessary to make people think about the meaning behind the words.

Breathe new life into familiar words:

- An unexpected picture with well-known words may surprise people into taking notice.

- A modern translation or a paraphrase such as the *'Living Bible'* or *'The Message'* can shed fresh light on much-used passages.

- Find new treasures by exploring the Bible for yourself. Don't get stuck in a rut with a few key verses. If you are excited about a discovery you have made, your enthusiasm will spill over into your poster.

Well-known words with an
unexpected picture.

Interpreting the Bible for today's world

Expressions in the Bible that were clearly understood by their original readers may need extra clarification today. For instance, how would the recipients of Paul's letter to the *Philippians* have interpreted the word *'citizenship'* *(chapter 3, verse 20)*? Philippi was a colony of Rome and its inhabitants were all too well aware of the privileges and special status of Roman citizens. To understand Paul's use of the word 'citizenship', read *Acts 16:37-39* and see how acutely embarrassed the magistrates of Philippi were, when they discovered that Paul was a Roman citizen after they had had him publicly flogged and thrown into prison without a trial.

On a poster it is not possible to explain all the background to a phrase such as *'citizenship in heaven'*. Sometimes it is better to find a present-day (and local) equivalent. For example, in Jersey, where there are restrictions on property-buying for newcomers to the island, the expression *'housing qualifications in heaven'* might be more appropriate!

'In my Father's house are many rooms.' (John 14:2)

2   THE COMMISSION OF THE POSTER-MAKER

'...our gospel came to you not simply with words, but also with power, with the Holy Spirit and with deep conviction.' I Thessalonians 1:5

Our message needs to carry conviction. If you have doubts about poster-making, ask God to confirm that this is his plan for you. He may do this by giving you a new enthusiasm and fresh ideas for posters, or through the encouragement of Christian friends, or through a Bible verse. Look up *Mark 16:15* or *Isaiah 40:9* or *Colossians 1:25-27*. Remember, it is God's work you are doing and the responsibility for the outcome is his.

Be true to yourself

The words you use will depend on your own circumstances. Be true to yourself but aware of your limitations. Don't try to be clever, using long words where short ones will do. Use Bible verses that you have found to be true in your own experience. If your faith and commitment to God are real, let them shine through. Your efforts to be clever will obscure God, rather than reveal him.

Whatever your message, spend time getting the words right. If you are not sure about grammar or spelling, be humble enough to ask a friend to help you. (Choose someone who will not dampen your enthusiasm.) Mistakes can be irritating to the person seeing the poster and distract attention from the actual message.

If you can, get hold of a good modern dictionary. You may make some interesting discoveries about words you thought you knew.

On one occasion (while thinking about *John 1:1*) I looked up 'word' in my Collins dictionary and was surprised to find a list of common phrases that gave me several poster ideas:

Have a word... (with Jesus)
(God) **sent word**
(God) **gave the Word**
(God) **gives his Word**
(God) **keeps his Word**
(God) **is as good as his Word**
In a Word... (Jesus)
My Word!
(Jesus is) **a man of his word**
(Jesus) **puts in a good word**
(for us) – see *1 John 2:1*
Take (Jesus) **at his word**
Take (Jesus') **word for it**
(Jesus) **is the last Word...**
(The Bible) **has the last word**

Explore the dictionary.

Everyday expressions on the church notice-board, especially if they have a double meaning, will attract attention because they are not what people expect to see.

Keep it simple

The simpler the message, the less chance there is of being misunderstood. Try to get to the heart of the matter, and avoid being obscure or controversial (unless there is good reason). Be willing to give up a cherished idea if necessary.

We can distort the truth by adding our own cultural overlay to the gospel. Your church denomination, your upbringing, the circle of friends you associate with, the newspapers you read and the television programmes you watch will all have influenced your attitudes and the language you use. Be aware of any bias you have, and of any special vocabulary that may have developed in your church that sounds strange to people outside.

What about the unpalatable truth?

The church poster-board is no place to air your grievances. However, the fact that a subject is unpopular should not deter us from raising it, if it is important.

For example, the need for repentance has never been easy to accept. Yet it was a priority for John the Baptist *(Mark 1:4)*, Jesus himself *(Mark 1:15)* and Peter *(Acts 2:38)*, and should still be so for us.

The unpalatable truth.

Marginal issues, over which Christians are themselves divided, are best left alone. When delivering an unpopular message, visual interest, colour and humour can help to ensure that the words are read, if not acted upon.

The local church

The message that is right for one church may not be appropriate for another. The choice of subject matter will be determined partly by the interests and abilities of individual poster-makers, and partly by the attitudes of the congregation as a whole. The location of the building will also need to be taken into account. A jocular catch-phrase that suits the modern town centre may be inappropriate for an ancient village church. Most important of all, the message must be suitable for those who are going to read it.

3   THE CONNECTION WITH THE POSTER-VIEWER

You may have a thorough knowledge of the Bible, strong convictions and a good understanding of your strengths and weaknesses, but if you cannot make your message accessible to people outside the church, you will be wasting your time.

Who is going to see the poster?

The difficulty is that each person's need is different. How can we cater for male and female, black and white, local and foreign, young and old, Christian, Muslim and atheist? To a large extent we must rely on the Holy Spirit to draw the attention of individuals to the poster that will help them most (hence the importance of variety and regular changes). And we must pray for guidance as to when we should display each poster.

However, we must also do our homework. First decide whether you are aiming primarily at non-Christians or Christians. If evangelism is the objective, analyse which are the main groups of people who regularly pass your church: commuters, shoppers, tourists, students, business people, shop assistants, factory or farm workers...? What are the particular concerns of each group? Target the needs of specific types of people.

Look at each poster you have made from the point of view of non-churchgoers seeing it for the first time. Ask yourself:

- Will they notice it?
- Will they understand it?
- Will they remember it?
- Will they respond to it?

Will they notice it?

Avoid wordiness. All we can expect is a casual glance, so words must be carefully chosen for maximum impact. Aim for something like a newspaper headline. Extra information can be added in smaller writing underneath, but your first priority, like the newspaper editor's, is to grab attention.

Words and picture must be absorbed in about six seconds. Once the message is lodged in the memory, it can be digested at leisure. As a general rule, ten words should be the maximum. Five would be better.

Watch the reactions of people passing in the street. If your poster is not noticed, it may be the look, rather than the message, which is at fault. Hints on design will follow in later chapters.

Will they understand it?

Passers-by need to see some connection with their own experience. We must provide the link, showing that God is not just the God of first-century rural Palestine. Jesus told stories about farmers and shepherds and village weddings because those were the things his listeners were interested in. Our themes and vocabulary need to be in tune with a society that is more at home with computer networks and international travel.

John chapter 1 gives examples of three different ways of telling someone about Jesus:

1 The simplest is Philip's direct invitation *'Come and see' (verse 46)*. There are times when a publicity poster, inviting people to a specific event, will be the most effective form of evangelism.

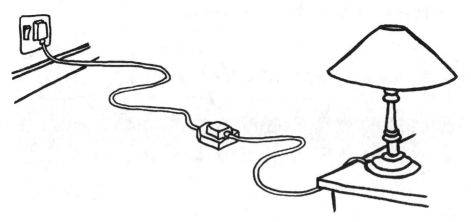

Making the connection.

2 In *verse 41*, Andrew's *'We have found the Messiah'* provided a link by showing that what was being offered was what his brother was looking for. Poster-makers, too, can find ways of demonstrating how Jesus answers people's needs, even those as yet unrecognised.

3 While some people need a very simple message, others are looking for something subtle and intriguing. John the Baptist's allusion to *'the Lamb of God'(verse 29)*, though familiar to us, must have surprised people the first time they heard it. The words are simple enough, but there is an interesting paradox between the word *'lamb'* (with its associations of gentleness, submission and vulnerability) and the word *'God'* (all-powerful, all-knowing, all-seeing). John the Baptist's words held additional shades of meaning for his original audience, who understood the significance of the Passover Lamb. We too can choose words appropriate to our culture, which raise questions or set the imagination working.

Will they remember it?

To avoid instantly-forgettable posters, try using the following:

1 **Questions** encourage people to think. Dogmatic assertions (especially negative ones: *'You must not...'*) reinforce rebellious attitudes and often produce a reaction opposite to the one intended.

2 **Riddles, proverbs and enigmatic sayings** are ways of arousing interest and curiosity. If Jesus had simply said *'It is hard for a rich man to enter the kingdom of heaven',* the words would have been quickly forgotten. What fixed the idea in people's minds was the ridiculous prospect of a camel trying to squeeze through the eye of a needle. Look at the book of Proverbs for more examples.

3 **Humour** is one of the poster-maker's most effective weapons. But it can cause hurt, so use it prayerfully.

4 **Puns, wordplay and well-known expressions used in an unexpected context** can all help to make posters memorable.

Wordplay.

Will they respond?

There is no way of predicting what each individual's reaction will be, but you can increase the chances of a positive response by avoiding:

1 **Jargon.** Avoid churchy jargon that means nothing to non-Christians. Words like *'saviour'*, *'atonement'* and *'sanctification'* are familiar in church sermons but not in common conversation. Others have a specific meaning for Christians that is different from the way they are used in everyday speech. For example, *'grace'*, normally means elegance or charm, rather than God's undeserved blessing. *'Sin'*, to most people, is murder or child abuse, (or a joke, as in the phrase *'living in sin'*), rather than rebellion against God. *'Election'* means voting for a politician, not God choosing us for salvation; and *'justification'* is more likely nowadays to mean adjusting a line of type (in printing) than a person being *'justified by faith'*.

   If there is a simple alternative for an unfamiliar word (like *'good news'* for *'gospel'*) then use it. The Authorized Version of the Bible may be beautiful to those who can understand it, but it puts unnecessary obstacles in the way of the average non-churchgoer. In some places, where archaic words have changed their meaning, it is actually misleading.

2 **A 'preachy' tone.** Beware of talking down to people or giving the impression that you know best what is good for them. Be sensitive to how people will react to what you are saying.

3 **Propaganda.** Our job is to communicate, not to manipulate. Don't be too influenced by the techniques of secular advertising. Aim for truthful simplicity and leave the Holy Spirit to do the rest.

4 **Trivialising the gospel.** Posters can be simple without being banal. The distinction is hard to define, but an example might be the difference between the

words *'God is love'* decorated with pink hearts on Valentine's Day, and the effect of the same words with a nail-pierced hand.

5   **Irrelevance.** Information is only useful if it has some significance for the person receiving it. In one of his books, Michael Green describes seeing a poster proclaiming *'JESUS IS THE ANSWER'*, on which some passer-by had scribbled *'but what is the question?'*

Only with God's help can we sense the real needs of those around us. Posters that are too general will not touch a chord of personal recognition or provoke any response.

IN A NUTSHELL

Our aim is to present the gospel in a nutshell, but we must make sure the kernel of truth is fresh, accessible and not so neatly packaged that there is no room for question or discussion. Words can arouse interest and stir the imagination, or they can reduce Christianity to a set of rules.

A good poster opens up new possibilities, like a book that leaves you at the end of one chapter eager to read on.

8 The picture

Pictures can speak louder than words

Of all the posters you have seen, which do you remember most vividly? What was it that caught your attention and remained imprinted on your memory? Although the words are important, the image is usually what fixes the idea in your mind.

Words need something to make them stick. Poetry and song have long been used as memory aids – at least since the time of Moses. (See the *Song of Moses* in *Exodus 15.*) But visual aids can be more effective in today's fast-moving culture.

The written word, on its own, has other limitations. It requires language and reading skills, whereas a picture can by-pass intellectual barriers, being interpreted in a more immediate and intuitive way.

First attract attention!

However good the message, a poster will achieve nothing if it does not first catch the eye. The visual impression is of vital importance.

There are various ways of making a poster look interesting. You may use an actual

... no room for coffee cups.

picture, made with collage, paint, markers, prints or photographs. Sometimes the words themselves provide the pictorial element, as described in the next chapter. Or interest can be generated with an unusual background or a surprising layout.

Our society is bombarded with words. News, publicity, information, instruction and advice drop through the letterbox and accumulate on the coffee table until there's no room left for coffee cups. Then we feel guilty because we haven't time to read it all! Let's find ways of using pictures to economise on words.

Words and picture must work together

On a poster, words and picture should function as one entity, reinforcing one another and held together by a single idea.

The picture is not merely an illustration, an optional extra tacked on, but an integral part of the whole. Avoid small pictures dotted about the paper or tucked away in the corners. The other extreme is to lavish care and attention on the picture, and then spoil it by adding writing that looks like a hurried afterthought.

Plan the words and picture together, allowing them to overlap and flow into one another. The result will be a more interesting and cohesive design. Alternatively, make the picture fill the whole paper and superimpose the writing, using dark writing where the background is light and vice versa, to make sure it shows up.

Plan words and picture together.

So you think you can't draw?

Don't be put off making posters because you think you can't draw. Our God is a God of surprises and he can develop talents we never knew we had. The ability to draw only comes with practice. Give small children some coloured crayons and they will start scribbling and making random patterns without feeling compelled to make something other people will recognise. If you can shed your inhibitions and become a child again you will be able to learn as they do, from experience. Spend time 'doodling' as often as you can, with pencil, pen, crayon or paintbrush. You will soon find yourself gaining confidence and your drawing will improve.

You don't have to be an artist to make posters. The aim is to find a simple, direct way of communicating an idea. As you read on, you will find many easy techniques for poster-making. More important than drawing skill is an open mind, a prayerful attitude and a spirit of practical inventiveness.

COLLAGE

Collage means 'sticking'. It is a bold and effective method of poster-making for beginners. At its simplest it is a matter of cutting or tearing letters and shapes out of coloured paper and sticking them onto a background sheet of a contrasting colour. One advantage is that the pieces can be arranged and rearranged on the background until a satisfying layout is achieved, before being stuck down.

Collage encourages non-artists to lay down simple strong shapes instead of fiddling with fussy line drawings. A solid shape has more impact than an outline – it is recognisable from a distance and more likely to stay fixed in the memory.

Materials for collage are cheap and readily available. The one thing you have to buy is glue. You will also need a firm backing sheet to stick on to – wallpaper or the backs of old posters will do.

What are you going to stick on to this backing? You can use almost anything that will not be too thick or too heavy to be held by the glue. When you need something in a hurry for a particular poster it is not always easy to find what you want. So start collecting interesting oddments of paper and fabric.

Paper Collage

Wallpaper has interesting textures as well as colours. You might make a poster using different shades and textures of just one colour, but make sure the words stand out clearly. Wood-effect wallpaper can be used for a cross or a door, stone for a rock or wall.

Tissue paper can be crumpled before gluing. Or, for a smooth surface of clouds or sea that you can write over, tear the paper into strips and attach with spray glue.

Crêpe paper, stretched and curled, makes natural-looking leaves and petals. Apply a dab of glue but leave the edge loose. Look at some real flowers (or at least a photo) before you start, noticing what makes a poppy different from a rose, but also noting that no two poppies are quite the same. A touch of paint will make flowers look even more real.

TIP **Applying glue**

To make sure the glue is where you want it, apply it to the back of the item to be attached, rather than spreading it generally on the sheet you are attaching to. It is not always necessary to cover the item completely, but make sure there is sufficient glue around the edges, particularly at the corners.

Crêpe paper is also useful if you want to make a large rainbow. Cut a straight strip from a roll of each colour, cutting across the grain so the strips can be curved to shape.

Fluorescent paper. Avoid the old-fashioned 'special offer' look by tearing, mixing and overlapping different colours informally. How about red, orange and yellow paper flames for Pentecost?

Fluorescent paper makes other colours look dull beside it. Use one or the other, not both at once, unless you are sure you like the effect.

Metallic foil. Stick coloured foil on a black background to look like a stained-glass window. It does not need to be elaborate – a simple pattern of different-coloured squares and rectangles, leaving a narrow black border between each section, gives a modern look.

If you can't find (or can't afford) rolls of coloured foil, a good group activity for

Some ideas for foil 'windows'.

adults or children is to collect shiny sweet wrappers and used Christmas decorations. Tear them into small, even-sized pieces and sort into piles of red, blue, green, etc. Slight variations of colour and texture do not matter, as long as they are well mixed. Having marked out a simple design on a sheet of black paper, decide what colour each section should be and stick on the foil pieces so that they join or overlap. Make sure each section is completely covered but leave a black line between sections. (If the edges are ragged, tidy them up with a black marker or cut out the sections when dry and remount on a fresh sheet of black paper).

Another possibility, allowing greater subtlety and variation, is to paint ordinary cooking foil with coloured inks. Mix the ink with a little PVA glue to help it adhere to the shiny surface, paint it on and leave to dry before cutting the foil.

Coloured magazine photographs can be used in many ways. One method is similar to the group activity described above, though the result is different. Small pieces torn from magazine pictures are sorted into piles of different colours and then stuck on to an outline picture drawn on a sheet of paper. The picture must be simple and bold, without much detail – sky, sea and rocks, or hills and trees. The result, with random mingling of different shades of each colour, is surprisingly attractive, rather like an impressionist painting. For instance, pieces torn from a photo of a face would provide a range of interesting colours for rocky cliffs – colours that you would not necessarily think of using if you were painting the picture.

Lettering can be worked in as part of the picture or stuck on afterwards.

Mosaics use a similar but more precise technique. Squares, about one centimetre across, are neatly cut from a variety of different types and colours of paper, to imitate the 'tesserae' (square pieces of coloured stone) used in Roman mosaic floors. In this case, the squares are stuck down not quite touching one another, in curving lines to emphasise the shape of the design. If you are interested in trying this, borrow a book from the library and see how the Romans did it.

Newspaper. Look for unusual ways of using everyday materials. A cross roughly torn from a sheet of newspaper (perhaps diagonally across the page rather than straight…?) might attract attention more than one neatly cut from craft paper. A problem with newsprint (apart from black fingers) is that the paper quickly yellows in sunlight, leaving a poster which looks elderly instead of immediate. One solution is to photocopy the page and use the copy rather than actual newspaper. (The casual quickly-made look is not always as easy as it appears!)

Papier-mâché, is messy but fun – a way of building up a raised area on your poster. Tear up newspaper into small pieces, soak in water and squeeze out excess. Add wallpaper paste or PVA glue, and water if necessary, squeezing and kneading until the mixture feels mushy but sticky. Spread the papier-mâché within an outline marked out on a spare piece of wallpaper or card, moulding to the shape you want. When thoroughly dry, cut out and remount on a clean background.

Another method, which you may find easier, is to tear the newspaper into strips and paint each strip with paste or glue, before laying it on the area you want to cover, building up the shape gradually, layer by layer.

We once made a poster with a nicely-rounded papier-mâché dodo (painted and with some feathers stuck on) with the words *The dodo didn't think about eternity either*.

Paper sculpture. Shapes which stand away from the surface of the paper will get noticed. Build up simple shapes from cones and cylinders, curls and spirals of paper. Try playing with some pieces of paper and see what ideas occur to you. Storing such posters is a problem but it may be possible, with simple designs, to pin the shapes in position on the poster-board and then flatten them down for storage.

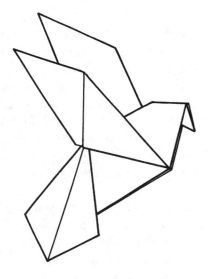

Origami bird.

Origami (Japanese paper-folding). Perhaps you already know how to make a water lily out of a paper serviette or a child's 'windmill' out of a square of coloured paper. If you fancy the idea of a folded paper bird, a fish or a frog, or a three-dimensional star for a Christmas poster, origami instruction books are easy to find. The angular, stylised shapes have a modern look, although the art dates back a thousand years. Origami paper is usually about six inches (fifteen centimetres) square but for a poster you will need an accurately-cut square of thin crisp paper three or four times that size.

Fortunately, the larger size makes the folding easier.

Tangram. Another idea for an unusual poster would be to use a tangram. This is an ancient Chinese puzzle, that is simple to make out of a square of card. It consists of seven geometrical shapes (five triangles, a square and a parallelogram), that can be arranged in hundreds of different combinations, to make abstract designs, animals, birds, fish, buildings, boats or people.

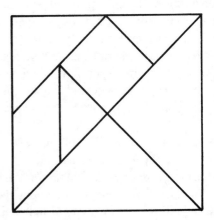

Tangram.

Collage with other materials

Don't be afraid to mix different materials together on one poster. A variety of textures makes it look more interesting.

Fabric. Poster-makers can use fabrics, as well as banner-makers. Experiment with the textures of velvet, satin, mohair, fur fabric, lace, net, corduroy, denim or hessian. Each has its own associations in our minds. Slippery, fraying materials may need backing with iron-on Vilene. Heavy cloth needs strong glue, staples or pins. Ribbons, braids, beads and sequins, even pieces of embroidery or tapestry, can find a place on the church poster-board, given the right occasion.

Tangram figures.

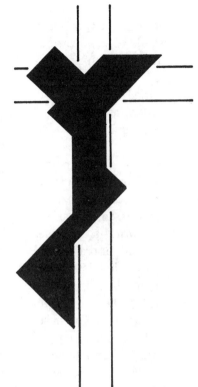

However, restraint is necessary. A poster dripping with satin, beads and sequins can look ridiculous. One element of brilliant colour (or unusual texture) on an otherwise plain poster is far more effective.

Remember the importance of contrast and variety. For example, the effect of Lurex or sequins is wasted on a bright background – they show up better on plain black. And fabrics should not be used too often. Any novel approach is best used occasionally, for special effect.

On the whole, bold patterns are less useful than plain fabrics. But at one of our workshops a thirteen-year-old made an interesting poster by cutting bright flowers from a discarded dress and sticking them informally on to a plain

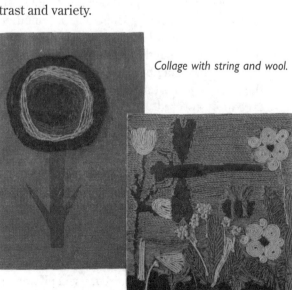

Collage with string and wool.

brown cross so that it looked as if the cross itself was sprouting new life.

String, rope and wools of various shades and thicknesses can be coiled and twirled into patterns of flowers and foliage, or rocks and sea.

Pulses, seeds, pasta, sand or gravel can all be used to make pictures. In front of me as I write is a dresser with jars of orange and brown lentils, green mung beans, purple kidney beans, cream coloured soup pasta and greyish pearl barley. I can imagine a poster, illustrating God's bountiful

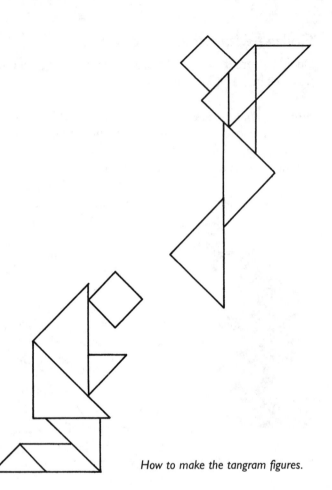

How to make the tangram figures.

goodness to us, with the shelf and the glass storage jars drawn or painted, but with real lentils, beans and pasta stuck on. Another idea comes from the cover of a past issue of TEAR Fund's magazine. It shows a map of Africa made out of sand, with a hand planting a single green seedling.

If you are using beans or large pasta, spread glue over a small area and stick on the pieces one at a time. With sand it is easier to spread glue liberally over the whole area to be covered. Pour the sand on while the glue is still wet and shake off any loose particles.

For more collage materials see page 110 *(Materials)*.

PRINTS

The purpose of the following suggestions is not large-scale reproduction, though designs can be repeated when more than one poster is needed. These are simply ideas which will add variety and interest to your posters, and are fun to try. If a large number of posters is required, use a photocopier or a professional printer.

Potato prints

Cut a large potato in half and, using a small sharp knife, carve away the parts you don't want to print. Shapes need to be simple and chunky. Apply fairly dry paint with a brush and try out the print on some scrap paper. If you don't like it, cut a slice off the potato and start again.

Cut house and roof separately if you want to print them in different colours.

A picture can be built up using a few basic shapes printed in a variety of colours – a garden of brightly-coloured flowers, for instance, or a village made up of houses, trees and a church. A decorative border can be created using crosses or zigzags repeated over and over again, but make sure the border complements the message rather than overpowering it.

Lino prints

Picasso used lino prints for posters and so can you. You will first need to visit an art shop and buy lino, cutting tools, printing ink and a small roller. Draw a simple design on the lino, then cut away the parts you don't want. Squeeze a small amount of printing colour onto an odd piece of glass, Formica or smooth card and roll until it is evenly spread on the roller. Roll colour all over the surface of the lino and place a sheet of clean paper on top. The best way of transferring the colour evenly is to roll firmly over the paper with a rolling pin (from the kitchen), or a second (clean) roller from the art shop. If neither of these is available, you may be able to improvise with a bottle or a section cut from an old broom handle.

Art shop lino is quite expensive, but you can take a large number of prints from each lino-cut. You might limit the cost by using a small piece of lino for the first print and then enlarging on the photocopier.

Leaf prints

Collect a variety of leaves, especially those with an interesting outline and a clear pattern of veins. Paint the underside of the leaf and press it down firmly on the paper. The results are unpredictable, so practise

Leaf prints.

first on spare paper, or choose only the best prints to cut out and remount. With children, have some fairly dry paint ready-mixed in pots, either a range of different greens or a selection of autumn colours.

Sponge printing

Use small pieces of sponge or foam rubber, dipped in paint, to produce a soft all-over pattern as a background for a poster. Dab gently, leaving open spaces between dabs, so the colour of the paper shows through.

A sponge is useful for printing cloud patterns too. Cut or tear off the square corners of synthetic sponges, or bunch up the sponge in your hand to create a more natural shape.

A paint roller

A small sponge roller, which is cheap to buy, can also be used for backgrounds. Don't attempt to cover the area uniformly, as you would if you were painting a wall, but vary the amount of pressure and leave patches of the original colour.

Another idea, for a large poster, is to create a townscape, rolling out rectangles of various heights and colours, for tower blocks and low-rise buildings. Add windows with a felt pen, brush or crayon, or print them with a stick of potato or carrot.

Hands, feet and fingers

Finger print.

Children love making prints of their own hands and feet. One St Paul's poster used hands printed in brown, black, pink, beige and tan, arranged in the shape of a cross, with the words *'We are all one in Christ'*. Footprints might illustrate the idea of coming to Jesus or following Jesus.

A single giant fingerprint (blown up several times on a photocopier) could show how God has made each human being unique; a set of fingerprints might be used with the words *'If you were accused of being a Christian, would there be enough evidence to convict you?'*

Wood

Odd pieces of wood, cotton reels, matchboxes and other scrap materials can all be used for prints. How about using a rectangular block of wood to print bricks for a wall, then adding a 'graffiti' message?

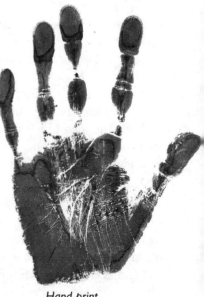

Hand print.

RUBBINGS

An easy alternative to leaf prints is leaf rubbings. Lay a sheet of paper over a leaf (vein-side up), hold it firmly so that it doesn't move about, and scribble lightly over the paper with a wax crayon, coloured pencil or carpenter's pencil.

Anything that is embossed or indented can make an interesting pattern. In church, take rubbings of metal gratings, mosaics, wood-block flooring and brickwork, as well as the more obvious carvings and inscriptions.

One of our poster-makers made a 'crazy paving' path from a variety of rubbings, with the words *'I will go before you and make the crooked places straight'.*

Path made from rubbings.

'RESIST' TECHNIQUES

Wax-resist

Draw a design on a sheet of paper, using a wax crayon or an ordinary household candle. Then paint a watercolour wash of a different colour over the whole surface. The surrounding area accepts the paint, while the wax resists it, retaining its original colour. Some lovely subtle effects can be achieved in this way. The technique might be appropriate for a poster about faith, using *2 Corinthians 4:18* or *5:7*, or *Hebrews 11:1*.

Masking fluid

If you want a crisp rather than a soft outline – for clear white lettering, perhaps – use masking fluid instead of wax. It is a yellowish solution sold in art shops for the purpose of masking off white areas of a watercolour painting. Using an old brush and washing it frequently, paint masking fluid over the areas you wish to remain white. Allow to dry, then apply a watercolour wash over the whole area. When the paint has dried, the rubbery film of masking fluid is removed, using your finger or a soft eraser.

Tie-dyeing

Tie-dyeing is another application of the 'resist' principle. You may have tried tie-dyeing fabric, but did you know that the process works equally well with paper? The piece of paper is crumpled, folded, pleated or gathered, then tied tightly, before being dipped into a bowl of dye, coloured ink or paint. The exposed parts of the bundle will absorb the dye while the tied areas do not.

The familiar 'sunburst' pattern can be achieved by gathering the paper from a central point, like a folded umbrella, (a pencil inside may help), then binding with string, thread or rubber bands. Extra variety is added by covering the point or other areas with polythene to resist the dye. Use tongs, rubber gloves or a polythene bag to protect your hands while dipping the sample into the dye. Soft absorbent papers only need a quick dip. Papers with special finishes will take longer. The bundle must be left to dry on newspaper before untying, as paper tears easily when wet. It can then be smoothed out by hand and carefully ironed to remove the creases.

An infinite variety of marbled, striped and criss-cross patterns can be produced by crumpling and folding the paper in different ways, but don't expect the results to be precise. The fun is in being ready for the unexpected! Even 'failures' may provide raw material for future posters.

Batik

This can also be done on paper. In this case, hot wax is applied to the area that you want to resist the dye, and then removed by ironing. Lovely effects can be produced this way, but as it is rather a specialised technique, find a book from the library for instructions.

PAINT

There are two ways of learning to paint. One is to pick up a brush and learn by trial and error. The other is to find a teacher. Either way, progress is only made by practising. There is a third group of people – those who would like to use paint but don't have the courage to try. If you are one of the timid ones, remember there are other ways of applying paint than with a brush. Ideas for prints and resist have already been described. Here are some other methods:

'Butterflies'

Children (and adults) love this. Prepare some containers of brightly-coloured runny paint (e.g. red, yellow and blue). Pour a small pool of each colour onto the paper, or apply it with a large brush. Fold the paper in half, spreading and mixing the paint as the two halves are pressed together. Open out and admire your beautiful butterfly (or nasty mess!) Keep trying till you have one you really like.

Spray cans

Spray can art has become a highly developed art-form on the subways of New York. If you can't afford an airbrush, it is surprising what can be done with a can of spray paint.

Make sure ventilation is adequate and avoid inhaling the spray. Spread newspaper or an old sheet over the area where you are spraying and practise on some scrap paper first. Soft misty skies, sea, hills and valleys can be created by moving the can backwards and forwards about a foot from the paper.

The picture can be made more interesting by masking off certain areas, so that the paint does not reach them. For example, tear out some cloud shapes and lay them on a sheet of white paper. Spray lightly over the whole area with a can of blue paint. When you remove the cloud shapes the place where they were will still be white.

If you want definite lines rather than an area of soft colour, hold the can close to the paper (but keep it moving).

Alternatives to the spray can

A cheap and environment-friendly alternative is a spray 'diffuser', which can be bought from an art shop. It is made of two tiny metal tubes hinged together. See page 117 *(Materials)*. One end is dipped into a bottle of ink or a jar of runny paint. Blow hard into the other end and the paint will come out as a fine spray. Take frequent breaths or this concentrated blowing may give you a headache. If you find it too hard, experiment with a perfume or garden spray.

The simplest method of all is spatter-painting with an old toothbrush. Dip the brush in ink or runny paint and scrape a knife quickly over the bristles towards you. Try laying a piece of fern or bracken on the paper, or some leaves, then spatter paint over them. You may need to fix them in place while you do this – if you put a sheet of corrugated cardboard under the paper, you can pin the leaves down with sewing pins. When you remove the leaves, you will be left with a white image on the paper.

Spatter-painting.

THE HUMAN FIGURE

The hardest thing to draw is a person. A human face, or a figure in action, can be the most effective way of drawing attention to your poster, but, badly drawn, they will make the poster look amateurish, even ridiculous.

Practise drawing real people, or from photographs. Ask a friend to pose in the position you choose so that you can see the angles of arms and legs and how the head is positioned. Time spent looking is as important as the time spent drawing. Three of the commonest mistakes are:

- placing eyes too high up (they should be mid-way between the top of the head and the chin)
- making the neck too narrow (it should be almost as wide as the face)
- making hands too small (they should be as big as the face).

If you want to practise at home, sit in front of a mirror and draw yourself.

Other ways of representing people

If your drawing skills are limited, find ways of conveying the impression of a person without too much detail. Here are some ideas:

Silhouettes or outlines without features reduce the likelihood of a figure looking comical when the subject is serious. The pictures in the Good News Bible are models of simplicity. Use them as a guide but, if you intend to copy them, write for permission to the Bible Society, Stonehill Green, Westlea, Swindon, Wiltshire SN5 7DG.

Stick men are easy; or invent simple cartoon characters.

Torn paper figures are informal and fun. Tear pieces of paper in a variety of bright colours into strips, ovals and oblongs for limbs, heads and bodies. Arrange the pieces on a background, moving them about like jointed puppets until you are satisfied with the

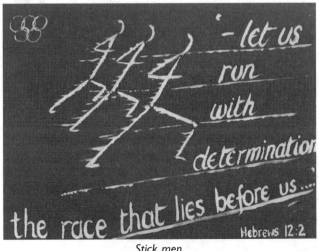

Stick men.

TORN PAPER

Torn paper figures.

positions of arms, legs and head. Experiment with people doing handstands, jumping, sitting, kneeling. Leaving a slight gap between parts of the body when you stick the figures down will increase the look of informality.

'Scribble' figures are quick and easy, using oil pastels, soft pastels, coloured pencils or crayons.

Photographs can be used in many ways. Enlarging colour photos to poster size is expensive, but black and white photocopies can give interesting results.

Be imaginative. Rather than just sticking the photo on a backing sheet and adding the writing underneath, try some of these ideas:

Scribble figures.

- **Superimpose words** on the photo or cut letters out of it.

- **Extend beyond the frame** of the picture by cutting away part of the background, allowing a pointing finger or a waving hand to stick out.

- **Cut the photo into strips** and stick down with slight gaps, even jumping some of the strips about to add life to the picture.

- **A composite picture** can be made with eyes, nose and mouth from different faces.

'WE LOVE...

BECAUSE HE FIRST **LOVED US'** I JOHN 4:19

Letters cut out of the picture.

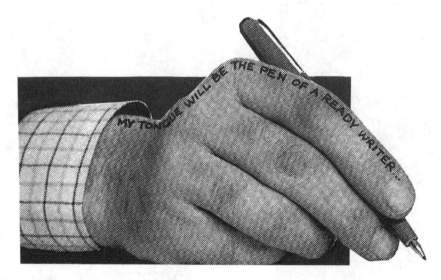

Words written on the photo.

ARE YOU READY TO GIVE YOUR SECURITY BLANKET TO JESUS?

Extending beyond the frame.

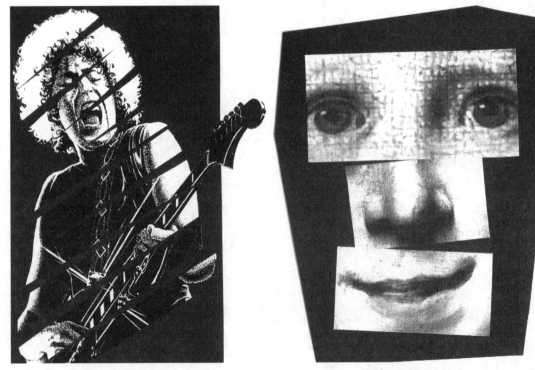

Photo cut into strips.

Composite picture.

Before using photographs of people, make sure you have permission from both photographer and subject, or from the publisher.

'Posterisation' is a technique that uses areas of solid colour to indicate shape, rather than outlines or shading. To do this, you will need a black and white photo with strong contrasts of light and shade. The aim is to produce a simplified version of the picture, using only two colours, one dark and one light. The easiest way is to enlarge the photo on a photocopier first, to the size you want. Place a sheet of tracing paper over the photocopy and outline either the dark or the light areas. (If the picture is mainly dark, concentrate on the light parts; if it is mainly light, pick out the dark areas.) It is easy to get distracted by what you think you should be drawing (eg the shape of the eye rather than the shape of the shadow). If this is a problem, try turning the photo round so you are drawing it upside-down. This

POSTERISATION

1 Photo with strong contrasts.

2 Outline light or dark areas.

3 Fill in the dark areas.

4 Finished picture.

sounds strange but it will help you to focus on the actual shapes rather than the features they represent.

Transfer the drawing from the tracing paper to the poster by scribbling on the back. See page 82 *(The Lettering)*. At this stage the picture will be barely recognisable, but don't give up. Finally, colour the dark and light areas, using black and white, or purple and yellow... or whatever you fancy.

The figure of Jesus

Avoid painting or drawing Jesus' face, unless you are sure it is right to do so. The result is almost bound to be disappointing. If your poster really needs the figure of Jesus, use a silhouette, an outline or a back view; or perhaps his hands, his feet, or his footprints.

You might get round the difficulty by using the word JESUS or a biblical symbol such as the manger, the cross, light or bread, a lion or a lamb. You could use a picture of something else to illustrate one of Jesus' attributes – the sun to represent the warmth of his love, a zigzag of lightning to show his power, a great rock for his dependability. Or simply imply his presence by showing Christians kneeling in prayer or with hands raised in praise.

COPYRIGHT AND CLIP ART

If you are not confident about your own artistic ability, it is tempting to use someone else's drawing, especially if you have access to a photocopier. But if a professional artist sees his work on your church notice-board without permission, you can expect him to be justifiably annoyed. Artists have a right to be paid for their work and if you copy their drawings, on a photocopier or by hand, without asking permission, you are in effect stealing from them.

Fortunately, a large selection of copyright-free material is now available, in book form or on computer disc. When you buy the book or disc, you buy the right to copy the material. The system, known as 'clip art', is very simple. There is no need to cut up the clip art book. Photocopy the page you want, then use the photocopy in whatever way you like – eliminating parts of the drawing you don't want (by cutting or with Tipp-Ex), enlarging (several times if necessary), arranging the result on a clean sheet of paper and re-photocopying. Add lettering and colour to suit the needs of the poster.

Using clip art is so easy that one is tempted to become lazy. Rather than being satisfied with a picture that is nearly right, find ways of combining parts of one picture with another or grouping figures in different ways to achieve exactly the effect you want. For more about copying and enlarging, see page 81 *(Lettering)*.

A list of **CLIP ART SOURCES** can be found at the end of this book.

Design your own maze.

PUZZLES

Puzzles can stimulate curiosity and encourage active participation.

Try writing your message on the squares of a crossword puzzle or a scrabble board. Or hide a Bible verse among a jumble of other letters like a wordsearch puzzle. (Circle the relevant words in a different colour to make it easier!)

Make your picture look like a jigsaw puzzle with one piece missing, or use a tangram (described earlier). A maze could illustrate Jesus' words *'I am the Way'*. How about a game of noughts and crosses with the words *'Choose the cross…'*? Or can you find an appropriate message to use with the traditional hopscotch grid?

Writing words in code is another way of arousing curiosity, but make sure it is not too difficult to decipher. Use code for part of the message only, so that the meaning can be deduced from the remaining words. Or have the same poster on adjacent notice-boards, with one message in code and one in normal writing. A children's code book from the library will give you plenty of ideas – try Morse, semaphore, Braille, signal flags or sign language as used by the deaf. What about a series of messages with the word *'Jesus'* in a different code each time?

BE SPECIFIC

Whatever method you use, don't try to cover your lack of self-confidence by being vague. The person seeing the poster needs to know what your drawing represents. Instant recognition of the picture is the key to quick understanding of the message.

If you are not sure what a donkey looks like, it is tempting to sketch a nebulous shape with a head, two ears and four legs and hope people will guess what it is. Instead, try to find some pictures (or a real animal) and see what makes a donkey look like a donkey.

A poster that focuses on something specific is more effective than one that is too general. Instead of painting 'a flower', think whether it should be a bluebell, apple blossom or a Christmas poinsettia. Each brings to mind associated ideas, which add interest to the poster.

Use your own experience and make posters about the things you know. If telephones and computers are more your line than donkeys and apple blossom, then use them for your posters. Practise drawing, not from memory, but from actual objects. As you learn to look at things around you, your drawing will improve.

FIND PRESENT-DAY IMAGES

'I press on... to win the prize'.
Philippians 3:14

Avoid predictable images that have become clichés, or find fresh ways of using them. A Victorian engraving of Jesus the Good Shepherd, which is comfortingly familiar, will not jolt people into considering what Jesus actually meant. Instead, find a photograph of a Bedouin in present-day Israel, or a newspaper picture of local sheep-dog trials. Or use the traditional image as a backdrop to crates of sheep waiting to be sent to the slaughterhouse.

When Paul wrote 'I press on towards the goal to win the prize' (in Philippians 3:14), the prize he was thinking of was probably a laurel wreath. A silver cup or a gold medal would be a more appropriate picture for us. When he described the armour of God (Ephesians 6:11-17), he had a Roman soldier in mind. A more accessible image today might be of riot police with fibreglass helmets, fireproof suits, batons and plastic shields.

Jesus used illustrations of sheep and vines and figs, familiar to people living in a simple rural community. Had he lived today, he might have talked of videos and supermarket trolleys and fax machines. Use everyday objects to illustrate spiritual truths and you will be following in the footsteps of Jesus.

9 The lettering

Letters can be fun!

Are you a person who enjoys making pictures but is afraid of spoiling the poster when you add the writing? Take heart. You do not have to be a sign-writer or an expert in calligraphy to be able to make interesting and readable letters.

Posters give scope for a bit of fun, provided you don't have too many words. Books are different. The text of a book must be consistent and clear, but for a poster the first priority is to attract attention. Letters have more chance of doing this if they have a character of their own than if they are dull and predictable. The enjoyment comes in drawing letters that express your individuality.

Have you ever considered how amazing it is that signatures can be used for identification? Yet in spite of this almost infinite variety in styles of handwriting, we are still able to read what has been written. Strangely, while handwriting shows so much variation, formal lettering has hardly changed since Roman times.

Like the clothes we wear, the letters we create reflect our personality and our taste. But, just as we choose appropriate clothes for different occasions, the style of writing must suit the subject. The shape, the size, the colour and the arrangement can enhance or contradict the message of the poster.

And, of course, the letters must be readable. An 'A' must be clearly an 'A'; an 'S' must not be confused with a '5'. If the message cannot be read, it will not be taken to heart.

In a world where eyes have become attuned to the printed word, they easily pick up irregularities in any writing that tries to imitate printing. So you have two alternatives. Either choose a form of lettering that is obviously intended to be free and informal, where the letters look interesting precisely because they are not all exactly the same. Or use aids such as the computer and the photocopier, dry transfer letters, stencils and clip art, to make sure the results look professional and neat. The one thing to avoid is a poster that looks as if it did not quite succeed in what it set out to do.

Aim for simplicity and be prepared to experiment, as you try out some of the following.

INFORMAL LETTERING

Using marker pens

Sausage alphabet. If you're nervous about drawing letters by hand, this is a good place to start, because sausage letters really are easy. They are also extremely adaptable, because they can be squeezed and stretched to fit almost any shape.

Use skeleton letters to draw round at first, if you are uncertain. Once you are happy with the basic fluid shapes and rounded corners, you can experiment and create your own variations. Letters can be squarish and chunky, very fat, thin and wavy, pear-shaped or whatever you like.

The outline can be filled in with the same or a different colour, or shaded with lines or dots. Overlapped letters make a pleasant design but can be difficult to read, so make sure the shape of each letter is clearly defined.

Typewriter. This is an interesting variation on standard primary school 'printing'. The addition of serifs transforms it into a lively and informal style that does not need to be controlled and neat to look good. If you're not sure where to put the serifs (the finishing-off strokes at the ends of the letters), get a typewritten page enlarged on a photocopier, so you can see the letters clearly.

Dot-to-dot. This has blobs instead of serifs. Jump the letters up and down for a light-hearted look.

Ladder writing. Often used for sketch-boards in street evangelism, this technique is easily adapted for posters. Draw two parallel lines and divide the strip into boxes. By blocking out appropriate areas in each box you can make simplified capital letters.

SNIPPED SQUARES

SPLIT SQUARES

RANSOM NOTE

torn letters

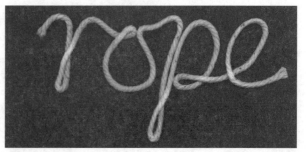

Handwriting. If your handwriting is pleasant and easy to read, use it occasionally to add variety to your posters, especially as a contrast to formal lettering.

Using scissors and glue

Snipped squares. Cut out squares of paper or card (or use adhesive labels), in a colour that contrasts strongly with the background. Snip away small pieces to make chunky capital letters.

Split squares. Cut squares of card into two or more pieces in such a way that, when separated slightly and laid on a contrasting background, the empty space between the cut edges forms a letter.

Ransom note. Printed letters can be cut at random from headlines and advertisements in magazines (rather than newspapers which discolour quickly) and stuck down to look like a ransom note.

Old posters. Cut letters and words from printed posters and re-use them in different ways.

Collage. Fill in a huge outline letter with small pieces of torn paper or foil, or with pasta, lentils, gravel, etc... (using strong glue!)

Cut-out letters. Letters can be drawn freehand, or using a template, onto wallpaper, wrapping paper, foil or fabric and then cut out and stuck onto the poster.

Torn letters. For a casual look, tear the letters instead of cutting them.

String, rope or thick wool can be formed into letters and stuck onto the background with strong glue. Loopy 'cursive' writing is most suitable.

Other techniques

Templates. These are letters used as a pattern to draw round. Make your own by cutting letters out of card. If you make a complete alphabet, they can be used over and over again for different posters.

Spray paint can be used graffiti-style (holding the can close to the paper and keeping it moving) or spraying over templates so that the letters remain the colour of the background while the surrounding area changes colour.

Wax-resist techniques, described in the last chapter (page 59), can also be used for the writing. Use masking fluid (obtainable from art shops) if you want the writing to be clear and precise.

Printing. Try potato prints or, for a set of letters you can store and reuse, make your own rubber stamps out of ordinary pencil erasers. Draw each letter (in reverse) on a separate rubber and cut away the part you don't want to print, using lino-cutting tools or a sharp craft knife.

Raised lettering. Another way of printing, if you want several copies of the same poster, is to build up a raised design, in reverse, by cutting simple bold letters out of card and sticking them on to a firm backing sheet. You will need a tube of oil-based printing ink and a roller. To print your design, follow the same procedure as for lino prints. See page 57 (*The Picture*).

Try cutting the letters out of textured wallpaper or fabric for interesting effects.

With any method of printing, *remember to design your letters back to front!*

Rubbings. A less messy way of reproducing a raised design is to take rubbings from it, using a thick wax crayon. In that case, draw your letters the right way round (not in reverse).

Three-dimensional letters

- **Polystyrene ceiling tiles** are easy to cut cleanly if you use a simple battery-operated tool obtainable from do-it-yourself shops. The letters can be left white or painted, and stuck onto your poster, but test both paint and glue on a spare piece of polystyrene first, as some substances cause it to melt away!

- **Corrugated cardboard** letters require strong scissors or a sharp knife. Layers can be built up to give depth to the composition. The ribbed surface adds texture and interest so, if your cardboard is smooth on both sides, try peeling off the top layer.

- **Glue 'piping'** is fun, if you want to try something really different. If you have PVA glue in a container that has a nozzle, use it as you would an icing nozzle for writing on a cake. It takes a bit of practice because you have to control the flow and keep the movement steady, but if you find you can do it, mix the glue with some ink or powder paint (otherwise it dries colourless) and pipe away!

FORMAL LETTERING

When a large amount of information is needed on a publicity poster, clarity is vital. Even with printed letters, reading will be slowed down if you choose a typeface that is too ornate or unusual. The basic information ('what', 'where' and 'when') must be absolutely clear and you cannot afford too many flights of fancy.

The computer

Computers have enabled non-specialists to produce immaculate lettering, speedily and efficiently, in a huge variety of styles. However, there are limitations, the main one being paper size. The standard home or office printer uses only A4 paper so, to make a larger poster, you either have to stick sheets together or enlarge the lettering on a photocopier.

If you do not have access to a computer, perhaps you can enlist the help of another church member to produce the text for you, when you need information clearly presented. If you find someone who is willing to do it regularly, ask them to print out some sample alphabets for you, showing all the available typefaces.

In order not to waste too much of this person's time, it may be helpful if you specify:

- which typeface you want (remember, chunky letters stand out better than delicate ones)
- whether the text is to be centred, or aligned left or right
- which parts should be bold, italic or capitals.

Also, rather than trying to produce text that is the right size for your poster, ask your colleague simply to print the whole thing A4 size, leaving you to enlarge it on a photocopier. This is easier for him and gives you a chance to cut it up and rearrange it if you wish.

If you have a computer yourself, spend time exploring its potential, finding imaginative ways of using it. If you are busy, it is easy to get into a rut, producing posters that always look the same. On the other hand, don't get too carried away with the novelty typefaces. They are eye-catching and fun to use, but can be quite irritating for the reader. Be aware that unusual typefaces go in and out of fashion and can quickly look dated. Some are also very difficult to read. If you do use a novel typeface, choose one that will enhance the message rather than distracting attention from it. And don't be half-hearted about it. Use it for just a few words (eg the title), make it big, and focus attention on it by keeping the rest of the lettering very simple.

A traditional typeface is likely to be easy to read but dull, unless you can find an unusual way of arranging the words. For greater impact, try combining it with paint or collage.

Dry transfer rub-down lettering

If you have never used it, buy a small sheet to experiment with. The procedure is simple:

1 Rule a faint pencil line across the full width of your paper. (The guide-lines on the transfer sheet are sometimes at the outer edges).

2 Select your first letter, position it carefully, then scribble all over it with a ball point pen or a not-too-sharp pencil.

3 Lift the sheet carefully, making sure the letter has transferred to the paper.

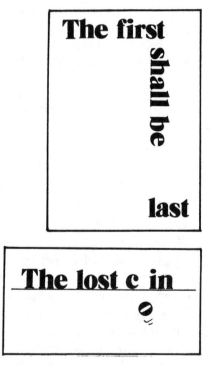

Dry transfer lettering – experiment and have fun!

4   If you need to make a correction, the letter can be lifted using Blu-tack or masking tape, or scraped off gently with a sharp knife.
5   To fix, cover with the protective backing sheet and burnish lightly with a spoon handle or fingernail.

As you produce each perfect letter, you will wonder why you never tried this method before! However, if you stand back, the overall look of your work may leave you feeling slightly disappointed. The difficulty is in getting the layout right, especially when large amounts of information are required. (You cannot adjust and rearrange, as you can when drawing your own letters.) Keep the number of words to a minimum, and consider using a different method for certain parts of the poster. A complete contrast, such as handwriting, brush lettering or torn-paper letters, looks better than a style that is similar but not so neat.

Alternatively, rub down your letters onto a separate sheet of paper, which can be cut up and reorganised before being stuck on the poster. With this method, you can also save expense by using small letters and enlarging them on a photocopier, adjusting size, layout and spacing as you wish.

Where regularity is called for, the computer is the easiest option, but dry transfer lettering is fun to experiment with in other ways. Try overlapping the letters, turning them sideways, putting one inside another, curving or zigzagging the base line or allowing one letter to fall off it.

An initial letter from Dover's 'Decorative Celtic Alphabets'.

Clip art books

Clip art, described in the last chapter, can be used for lettering as well as pictures. First photocopy the page you want, then cut up the copy (not the book!) Enlarge where necessary and arrange the various elements on a sheet of white paper. When you are happy with the layout, stick down the letters and re-photocopy the whole thing. Clip art is useful for a single decorative letter, or for commonly-used words and phrases such as 'Welcome!' or 'Harvest Thanksgiving', which can be lifted from the book without alteration. But piecing together large amounts of information letter by letter from a clip art alphabet is time-consuming and fiddly.

Dover have a good range of copyright-free alphabets such as 'Art Nouveau', 'Art Deco' and 'Bold Headline', as well as wonderful ornamental initial letters. The *Palm Tree Instant Art* series are a useful source of words and phrases frequently needed for church publicity. See page 157 for CLIP ART SOURCES.

Stencils

Stencil lettering is a convenient and neat method for beginners but, like dry transfer, somewhat inflexible for large amounts of information. First, sketch the words freehand, faintly with a pencil, to see roughly how they fit on the poster. Then, if you can contain your impatience, stencil the words with a pencil, before going over them again with a pen. The intermediate pencil stage allows you time to consider the layout as well as the actual stencilling.

If you cannot find any interesting stencils in your local shops, you might consider making your own. Dover, in their *'Cut & Use Stencils'* series, have a book of twenty different alphabets, printed on stencil paper, ready to be cut out with a sharp knife (and a steady hand!) Alternatively, you can make a stencil of your own, using oiled card or stencil film. A characteristic feature of stencils is the 'bridges' that prevent the central pieces of letters such as 'O' and 'B' from falling out. If you design your own, make sure you include enough bridges, so that the whole thing doesn't fall apart the first time you use it.

One other point about the bridges is worth mentioning. In most cases, if you simply want neat lettering without drawing attention to the fact that you used a stencil, it is best to fill in the gaps left by the bridges, by hand, after lifting the stencil off the paper. However, if you want to emphasise the stencilled, 'packing case' look, then leave the gaps.

If you intend to use paint or ink, you need to dab it on, using a stencil brush, a small sponge or a ball of cotton wool. Another possibility is to spray paint or ink, preferably using a stencil specially cut for the purpose with all the words on one sheet. The best material for this is transparent masking film, which clings to the paper, giving clean edges to the letters and making bridges unnecessary. The method is to draw the

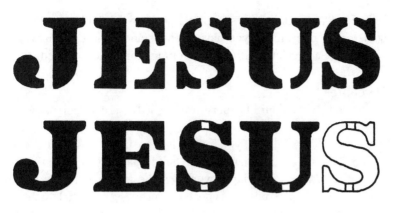

Fill in the gaps...unless you want to emphasise the fact that you used a stencil.

design on a spare sheet of paper, lay the masking film over the top and cut out the letters carefully with a scalpel or craft knife, following the lines showing through the film. Peel away the cut out letters, lay the stencil on the final background, making sure the surrounding area is well protected with newspaper, then spray. When the paint is dry, peel off the masking film.

Copying and enlarging

The photocopier

Many churches own their own photocopier. If yours doesn't, look around locally for a photocopying service that offers a good machine, a helpful operator and a sensible price. Libraries often have a photocopier which you can operate yourself but, as they are intended for reference rather than display, the quality may not be good enough for posters.

As mentioned in the last chapter, be careful about copyright. Do not photocopy lettering from books unless, like Dover Publications, they are designed for that purpose.

Nonetheless, the photocopier is invaluable as a means of enlarging computer output, dry transfer letters or clip art, as well as calligraphy done with a small pen.

If you have never used a photocopier, here are a few hints:

Designing the original

- Use white paper for the original. Copying from coloured paper produces a greyish background.
- If possible, use black lettering. On a basic photocopier, the letters come out black whatever colour you copy from, but some colours copy better than others (for instance, red works better than blue). Pencil lines will only show faintly, if at all.
- Photocopiers are not good at reproducing large areas of solid black. Try shading with lines or dots.
- If the design goes right to the edge of the paper, you will lose a few millimetres when it is photocopied.

- Paper for the original can be any size or shape up to A3 (297mm x 420mm), but A4 is usual. When enlarging, if you have used a standard size of paper (eg A4 or A5) it will be easier to calculate the amount of magnification needed.

Making the copies
- You can copy on to any colour of paper (or thin card) but dark colours will reduce legibility.
- Copies are normally A4 or A3. If you need a larger size than A3, start with an A3 original, fold it in two and enlarge each half separately. Then stick the two sections together. Allow for a slight overlap at the join or you may lose part of your design. For a larger poster, repeat the process and stick four sections together. Alternatively, photocopy strips of lettering and stick them on to a large coloured background.
- Enlarging magnifies small imperfections. You may need to tidy up some letters by hand.
- Photocopies are waterproof and resistant to fading, which is useful if you have an unprotected outdoor poster-board. Design your poster in black and white, photocopy it and then use oil pastel or waterproof paint to add colour.

The overhead projector

Do you have access to an overhead projector but not a photocopier? The OHP can be used as an aid to both copying and enlarging. To copy, place the sheet to be copied on the stage of the lighted projector, with a sheet of clean paper over it. The light will shine through, enabling you to trace the outline. To enlarge, trace the design onto an OHP acetate, then project it onto a large sheet of paper fixed to the wall, adjusting the angle of projection to avoid distortion.

Other copying methods

If you want to copy lettering, or a picture, accurately onto another sheet of paper, the traditional method is to trace the outline, using tracing paper (or greaseproof paper from the kitchen). Then scribble over the back of the tracing paper with a soft pencil, making sure you have covered the lines you want to reproduce. This produces the equivalent of carbon paper. Finally, lay the tracing, right side up, on your clean sheet of paper and draw over the outline firmly a second time using a sharp pencil or ball-point pen. If you are copying onto black paper, use a white pencil for the scribbling.

Buying a pack of carbon paper might sound easier, but most carbon paper is indelible, so mistakes cannot be erased. 'Trace-down' paper from an art shop is better, if you can find it.

One of the easiest solutions of all is to stick the original, covered by a sheet of clean paper, to a window or glass door so that the light shines through. Use masking tape to hold the paper firmly while you trace the outline. Or use a lamp under a glass-topped coffee table.

CALLIGRAPHY

Beautiful pen lettering can enhance a poster. But it is easy to get carried away with elaborate serifs and flourishes which obscure the message. Some letters, such as Gothic capitals, are so difficult to read that they are best avoided altogether, unless they can be radically simplified.

Gothic capitals are hard to read.

Where alternative forms exist, choose the one that is easier to read.

Aspiring calligraphers tend to be attracted by the unusual variations in historical alphabets. But where there are two versions of a letter, it is better to choose the one that is easily recognised by the modern reader.

Apart from the question of legibility, the main problem with calligraphy for posters is the difficulty of finding large enough pens. See page 114 *(Materials)* for some suggestions.

If you have never used an edged pen, don't expect to master the art without spending time practising. The first step is to join a class or get hold of a good book on calligraphy and work through it systematically. Each teacher has his or her own style, so find someone whose lettering you want to imitate.

The basic principle behind all lettering with a straight-edged pen (as opposed to the rounded nib of an ordinary fountain pen) is that the writer holds the straight edge of the nib at a constant angle to the writing line. This produces a consistent and rhythmical pattern of thick and thin strokes. Try holding the pen at an angle of 30° – that is, as if pointing to 11 o'clock. At this angle, the vertical strokes will be slightly thicker than the horizontal strokes.

Keep the edge of the nib at the same angle to the writing line.

The second important factor in pen lettering is using the correct width of nib for the size of lettering. Too narrow a nib results in weak, spindly letters, while letters written with too broad a nib lose their distinctive shape and become difficult to recognise. Calligraphy books always specify the correct number of nib widths for each style of writing. With experience you will be able to judge for yourself but at first it is best to follow the rules.

The third necessity is to acquire sufficient regularity in the forms of the letters to produce a harmonious pattern. This only comes with practice. Slight variations bring life to the page. Random inconsistencies are a distraction.

Fluency and rhythm will come with time but regularity of size can be quickly achieved by ruling pencil guide-lines. Most important are the tram-lines marking the top and bottom of the lower-case (small) letters. To begin with, you will also need extra lines above and below to mark the height of 'ascenders' and 'descenders' (the tops and tails of the letters). Extra time taken getting the proportions right will pay dividends later.

nib too fine

nib too broad

suitable nib

Guide-lines
help keep
lettering
regular

PICTURE LETTERS

As mentioned in the last chapter, the pictorial element of the poster is sometimes provided by the letters themselves:

Illuminated letters

An enlarged initial letter can be decorated in the style of a medieval manuscript, using a gold marker pen and paint in brilliant colours. If the decoration is elaborate, limit it to one letter, or the words become difficult to read. A modern initial letter might be entwined with flowers or have a person sitting on it (or leaning against it or looking through it). See pages 64 and 79.

Letters cut out of a picture

This technique reverses the normal process – the picture is inside the letters, instead of behind or alongside them. Choose a simple picture which can be understood even with bits cut out. It might be a large photograph from a calendar or an old poster, or a picture you have made yourself – a simple landscape, sky and sea, trees or massed buildings in a city. Make the letters chunky and squarish, with as little space as possible between them.

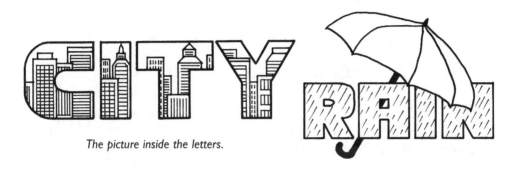

The picture inside the letters.

Letters that make the shape of the thing described

Letters can be compressed and elongated, curved and distorted, to make them illustrate the word used. The whole word or individual letters can make the shape.

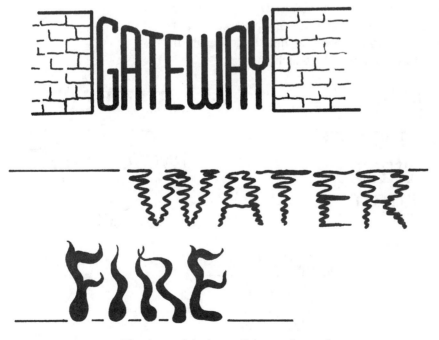

The shape of the letters illustrates the word.

Visual puns

It is possible to exploit double meanings to humorous effect by using (or leaving out) the letters themselves.

A visual pun (look carefully!)

SPACING

Line spacing

The distance between lines of writing can be varied to suit the meaning and the design. Leave enough space so that letters do not clash together, but not so much as to break up the flow of the text. A space two 'o' shapes high is safe, but you may prefer the look of closer spacing.

Several lines of equal spacing on a poster looks boring. Having reduced the number of words as far as possible, group words together in phrases, to offer the reader bite-size chunks instead of one solid mass. Leaving a large space after the first few words can be effective, allowing the viewer time to assimilate the picture before reading the punch line.

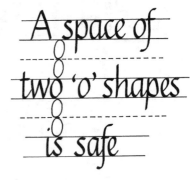

Word spacing

This is easy. Simply leave a space the size of an 'o' between words.

Letter spacing

With informal lettering styles the spacing is not too important, but when using dry transfer lettering or stencils, irregular letter spacing will be the first give-away of the amateur. The beginner frequently leaves too much space between letters. If they are packed fairly tightly together the result will look more professional.

The other mistake frequently made by the conscientious novice is to measure the distance between the letters. Unfortunately this does not work, because of the varied shapes. It is the area of space between the letters, rather than the linear distance, that has to be judged, and that can really only be done by eye. If you write out the word ILLUSTRATE (in large capitals) by measuring an equal distance between each of the letters, you will find that IL looks closer together than LL or LU. Look at the shapes of the spaces between the letters and you will see the differences in area. If you are a perfectionist, you may be disappointed to learn that there is no simple rule for letter spacing, but God has given us marvellously complex eyes and brains which can be trained to assess the amount of space needed. After a while you will find you are automatically adjusting your spacing as you write.

Word spacing.

LEGIBILITY

It is more important to be legible than to be clever. However eye-catching the poster, your work will be wasted if the words cannot be read.

Contrast

A common mistake is to use black lettering on a dark background, or yellow on white.

It is easier to read a solid letter than an outline.

PLEASE SHUT THE DOOR

Please shut the door

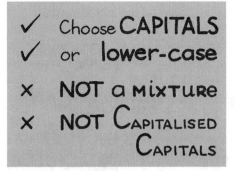

Writing cannot easily be read unless there is a strong contrast of dark on light or light on dark. Black lettering on white or on yellow gives the clearest contrast. White or yellow lettering on black is also clear but a little harder to achieve, because ordinary marker ink will not show up. Use opaque paint or cut-out letters. Many colour schemes give good legibility, but try a sample to make sure. If the poster is going to be displayed in a dark corner, strong contrasts are even more important.

Solid letters

From a distance, it is easier to read a solid letter than an outline, because empty space inside the outline confuses the eye.

Capitals and lower-case

Capital letters carry authority. Lower-case letters are friendlier and easier to read, because they give each word a distinctive shape. Choose one or the other but don't mix them in one word, unless you have a good reason for doing so. Capitals should all be the same height – generally speaking, you should not use a large capital followed by small capitals.

Size

Large letters are easier to read than small ones. The dimensions will be determined by the distance from which the poster is viewed, and the speed at which it is passed. People standing close to a notice-board can read small writing, but remember that those passing in a car will only be able to take in the message if the words are few and the letters large. Don't be afraid to *SHOUT* occasionally!

Vertical writing

This is difficult to read. We recognise words by the shapes of the spaces between the letters as well as by the letters themselves. If the letters are arranged one below the other, instead of side by side, the shapes between the letters are completely different. If you must write vertically, it may be best to turn the whole word on its side.

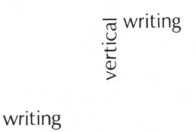

Variety

Make the poster easier to read by emphasising the most important words. Vary the size of the letters, as well as the weight (ie the thickness or boldness of the letters), but be careful to keep the thickness uniform within each word. Vary the style too. For instance, handwriting can be used to give an impression of speed or informality.

STYLE

Unity and simplicity

The importance of providing variety must be balanced against the need to keep the poster simple and clear. Do not introduce too many different styles of writing in one poster. Two is usually enough. Contrasting styles look better than two that are similar but not quite the same.

Make the style of lettering fit the content

To increase your awareness of the mood created by different styles of writing, try the following exercises, on your own or in a group:

TRY THIS EXERCISE

1 Gather a selection of brand names and logos, from advertisements and packaging, as well as titles from magazines and book jackets... Look at each one and ask, 'Why did the manufacturer choose this lettering style and how effective is it?'

2 Ask a friend with a computer to print a complete set of alphabets, showing all the available typefaces, large enough to see the differences clearly. Look at some of the more unusual typefaces one at a time and think what type of poster each would be suitable for.

3 Design your own letters to suit some of the following words, using pen, pencil, brush, or any other method described in this chapter:

ice	*sea*	*light*	*fire*	*speed*	*soft*
rain	*wood*	*faith*	*shade*	*fun*	*alive*

PUNCTUATION

On a poster, you should use as little punctuation as possible. Eliminate commas and full stops unless they are essential to the meaning. Instead, leave a gap between groups of words to create a pause, or else re-word the message to make punctuation unnecessary.

There are a few exceptions. If your poster asks a question, you must include a question mark. Exclamation marks may be used sparingly (but not peppered all over the poster to reinforce a weak message

or to show that you are joking). A single huge exclamation mark, or question mark, can make a dramatic focal point.

When a large space, or a picture, divides the message into two parts, a row of dots helps to lead the eye across the gap, because they imply that there is more to come.

Lead the eye...
across the gap.

If you want to make it clear that you are quoting directly from the Bible, or using Jesus' actual words, then use quotation marks (double or single), but it is not essential to do so. For example:

>   *Jesus said "I AM THE WAY"*
> OR   *Jesus said 'I AM THE WAY'*
> OR   *Jesus said I AM THE WAY.*

The apostrophe (the 'flying comma') is the only punctuation mark that regularly causes trouble for the poster-maker. The basic rules are fairly simple but, if in doubt, it is probably better to leave it out than to put one in the wrong place.

There are two occasions when an apostrophe is needed. The first is to show that something has been left out, as in *don't* for *do not*, and *I'm* for *I am*.

The second indicates possession, as in *Peter's boat* or *Jerusalem's walls* or *the disciples' faith*. For most people, the problem is deciding whether the apostrophe should come before the *s* or after it. Sometimes your decision will alter the meaning. For instance, *the disciple's faith* means there is only one disciple. *The disciples' faith* means there is more than one disciple.

If you want to be 100% accurate, look in your local library for a book on punctuation. But here is a simple rule that covers most cases:

>   If the word does not already end in *s*, add *'s*
>   (eg *the man's hat* or *the men's prayer group*)
>   If the word already ends in *s*, add an apostrophe after the *s*
>   (eg *the ladies' Bible study* or *Jesus' mother*).

There is just one example that nearly everyone finds confusing. When do you use *it's* and when *its*? In this case, you only use the apostrophe to show that something has been left out, not to show possession, (ie *it's* always means either *it is* or *it has*).

>   *It's* time to seek the Lord.
> BUT Don't let the world squeeze you into *its* mould.

FREEDOM AND DISCIPLINE

When you read about ruling guidelines for your lettering, you may feel it sounds like putting on a straitjacket. After all, what you want is to convey freedom, not rigidity. In fact, many hours of patient discipline may be needed before you can achieve those flowing lines that look so easy.

On the other hand, you may be comfortably settled into a risk-free rut, using the computer for all your posters, and the Lord may be saying 'Take up your brush and paint!' Whatever your temperament and whatever your level of expertise, keep moving on, experimenting and exploring new methods.

Remember that the form of the letters plays a decisive role in determining whether the words will be read or ignored.

10 Planning

Most people feel a strong temptation to leave out the preparation, and plunge straight into making their poster. However, a little forethought will lead to a better design, and save time and energy in the long run.

If you are painting a picture, you may be able to create a satisfying composition purely by instinct. But when lettering is involved, you must plan ahead – it is extremely frustrating to discover, too late, that you have not allowed enough space to finish a word. Well-designed lettering is interesting as well as easy to read. It may give an impression of being written at speed, but it should not look as if you couldn't be bothered to do it properly.

An organised layout does not need to lose its freshness. Learn to sketch out your ideas quickly and lightly and start work on the real thing before your enthusiasm and spontaneity have evaporated.

Instant success is something we have come to expect in an age of fast food and press-button entertainment. But that is not usually God's way of teaching us. Just as the musician needs to train his ear, so the poster-maker must train his eye to judge which layout will be most effective.

ATTRACTING ATTENTION

The first priority is to catch the eye. Here are nine key points to keep in mind when planning your poster:

1 **Size.** A large poster is more likely to be noticed than a small one, large writing than small.
2 **Colour.** Bright, strong colours make an impact and look exciting.
3 **Picture.** This is often the most important element, creating an instant impression and lingering in the mind afterwards.
4 **Contrast.** Strong contrasts increase drama. Writing must show up clearly against the background.
5 **Variety.** The style needs to be varied to keep posters interesting.
6 **Surprise.** Anything unexpected will attract attention – a commonplace item seen from an unusual viewpoint, an object precariously balanced as if it is about to fall, or something ridiculously out of scale (a huge ant stepping over a tiny house, perhaps). A hippopotamus wallowing on the church notice-board, or what appears to be an empty sheet of paper, will be more noticeable than a cross, which is what people expect to see.
7 **Simplicity.** Stick to one idea, one picture, few words.
8 **Position.** Will the poster be easily seen?
9 **Isolation.** Will it be competing with other notices and posters?

Finding the simplest method

Before you start, you need a clear idea of what you want to say and why. But when it comes to deciding how to make the poster, be flexible and open-minded.

The art of designing effective posters is to find the simplest way of achieving your purpose. A group of teenagers I worked with recently were set the difficult task of completing a poster in half an hour from start to finish. One of them, whose first idea was to depict 'growth' with a series of human figures from baby to adult, soon decided on the easier option of drawing a plant developing from seed to flower. Another girl used circles and rectangles cut out of gold foil and paper to represent a pile of money. Because the word 'money' was prominent in the message, this simple method worked well.

Be ruthless. Concentrate on one idea. Have the courage to discard all unnecessary words and any part of the design that does not contribute to the main aim. (You may find this difficult, especially if you are rather proud of the bit that needs to be left out!)

Make it easy to read

Generally, ten words should be the maximum. However, with a Bible verse, too drastic a reduction may alter the meaning. Even after eliminating all non-essential words, you may still have more than can easily be read at a glance. When that happens, find ways of arranging the text to help the reader:

1 **Group the words** into units of meaning.
2 **Vary the amount of space** between groups of words.
3 **Emphasise important words** by varying the size and weight.

TRY THIS EXERCISE

Find a sheet of paper and see what you can do with the following verse:

> *'Sow for yourselves righteousness,*
> *reap the fruit of unfailing love,*
> *and break up your unploughed ground;*
> *for it is time to seek the Lord*
> *until he comes*
> *and showers righteousness on you'. Hosea 10:12*

There are no right and wrong answers. Each person will approach the task from a different angle. Pick out the words you feel are important and arrange them so that they are easy to read. You will find three possible solutions on page 106 at the end of this chapter.

Which bit do I read first?

The order in which the words are to be read must be absolutely clear. By doing something clever with the design, you may be causing confusion for the reader.

Remember that the way we read is from left to right, and from the top to the bottom of the page. If the first word of your message is near the top left corner, the reader feels secure. If not, he or she is likely to be momentarily puzzled and may not bother to investigate further. If there are gaps, make sure they come at natural pauses.

How could these be made easier to read?

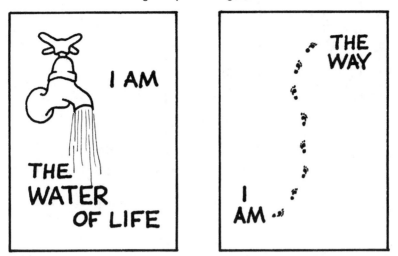

Leading the eye in the right direction.

Splitting the message into two halves can be effective – the first part to attract attention, the second to deliver the punch – but it must be obvious which part is to be read first. Where the sequence may not be quite clear, other devices can be used to lead the eye in the right direction: footprints, for instance, or running water (or even drips of blood!)

If you intend to arrange the writing in some unusual pattern such as a circle or the shape of a question mark, plan it carefully. The first words, in particular, need to be absolutely clear.

HOW TO PLAN

Rough sketches

Thumbnail sketches are an essential preliminary to poster-making. Have plenty of scrap paper handy. Offices discard mountains of paper that has only been used on one side. By re-using waste paper rather than buying a stylish sketchpad, not only will you be helping the environment, but you will feel less inhibited about trying out all sorts of ideas and throwing away those that don't work.

Ideas only take shape when you start to put them on paper. You may know what you want to do, but only discover how to do it by playing around with the component parts, rearranging and adapting them until they look right.

These first sketches can be quite small. Draw several boxes on a sheet of paper. If the finished poster has to be a certain shape (to fit a particular display-board), make sure your boxes are the same shape. It is no good planning your layout in an elongated rectangle if the finished poster has to be square, or designing it to fit an upright rectangle (described as 'portrait') if your display-board dictates a rectangle on its side ('landscape'). If the board is big enough, you can vary the size and shape of the posters for added interest.

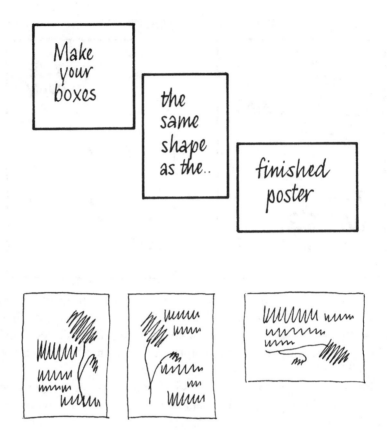

Quick scribbles to see how the different elements fit together.

Try out different arrangements.

Message Posters

Three simple ideas

*Painted background,
letters cut from strips of card.*

Oil pastels on blue card.

*Cut-out map and arrow, letters stencilled with
black marker.*

Torn fluorescent paper, foil, pastel and paint create a feeling of movement and excitement.

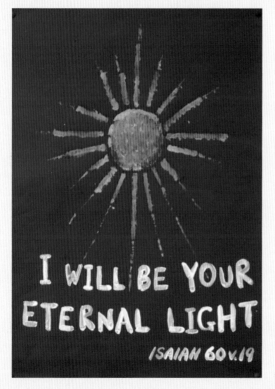

Four different ideas to express the word 'Light'

Sun 'printed' using pieces of wood.

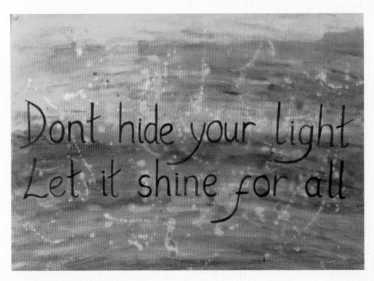

Background brush-painted,
then yellow paint flicked over it.
Lettering added with a marker when dry.

Big communal poster,
made by those attending the opening
of our new church centre.

Outline picture and letters drawn in advance.
Small pieces torn from magazines were stuck on by adults and children
throughout the afternoon.

THE IDEA 3

Ideas arising from difficult circumstances

Made by some whose only escape from family problems was in the bath!

Made after a frustrating day of unanswered phone calls.

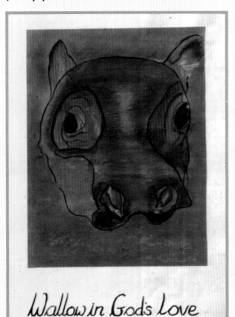

Wallow in God's Love

Pencil, pastel and charcoal.

Made after a tragedy at sea.

Paint, wallpaper and rub-down lettering.

COLLAGE

Cut strips of paper and card,
tissue paper petals, cut-out letters.

Sword made of folded card
covered with foil. Paper curled and torn
to look like ancient parchment.

Crêpe paper leaves,
and flowers cut from
pattered fabric.

COLLAGE

Marker, crayon and small pieces of 'holographic' shiny paper.

Torn paper figures.

Two posters made during a series of workshops on the Lord's Prayer

Sponge printed clouds, oil pastel rainbow.

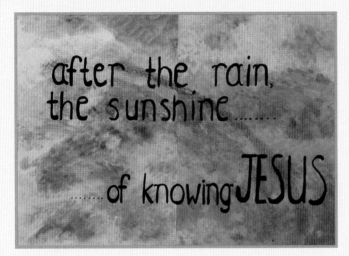

Hand prints using different coloured paint.

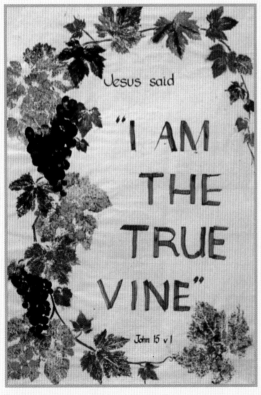

Leaves printed with real vine leaves, grapes printed with a cork and the red letters written with a piece of wood used like a pen.

PAINT

White spray 'printed' onto waves using small pieces of bobbly wallpaper, (used also for cut-out letters).

A lovely watercolour poster.
Did you spot the mistake?

Children's paintings cut-out and arranged
by an adult, who also added the words.

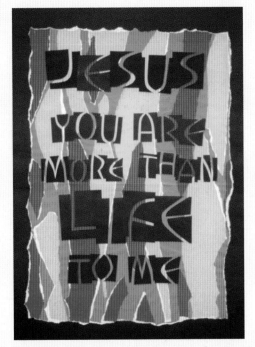

Split square letters on a background of torn strips of fluorescent paper.

Lively sausage letters cut from white card. (Sometimes it is better not to use a ruler!)

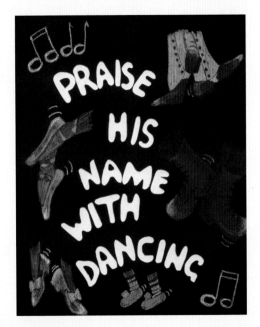

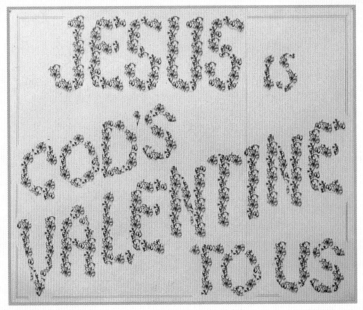

Letters cut out of floral wrapping paper.

PAINT, PEN AND RUB-DOWN LETTERS

Decorative lettering using thick and thin pens, on a sprayed paint background.

Dry transfer rub-down letters on watercolour.

Letters stencilled one at a time
with dryish paint to avoid smudging.
Bricks printed with a block of wood.

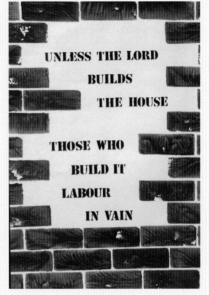

These mosaic letters and sea were made
using an 'Automatic' pen and paint, rather
than the usual cut squares.

Rub-down letters
and paint

PICTURE LETTERS

The vine makes the word.
Oil pastel and black marker

John 15 v 5

I am the vine

You are the branches

Jesus

ALL GOD'S PROMISES FIND THEIR **YES** IN CHRIST

II CORINTHIANS 1:20

Clouds sponge printed on painted sky before
cutting out letters.

12   THE LETTERING

Publicity Posters

Cut-out fruit and vegetables in vivid colours. Based on design of harvest invitations.
© CPO Worthing.

Flower bunches and a Christingle – clear images, with simple information that can be seen from a passing car.

Words printed with offcuts of wood.

Flowers cut from magazines and calendars. Lettering curved and waved to give variety.

Red and orange paper, torn and stuck together before letters were drawn and cut out. Coloured paper shapes in opposite corners add interest.

Bold titles, varied lettering styles and attractive layouts help the reader. Pictorial interest is added with the paint-box, foil flutes and starry sky.

Designing interesting posters with this much information is not easy. Prune if possible!

DIFFERENT TYPES OF POSTER-BOARD OUTSIDE SIX CHURCHES

Remember, these are sketches, not drawings. Don't waste time on detail or careful lettering. You may prefer to shade in quickly the shapes created by the picture and the words, (rather than actually drawing and writing), to see how they balance one another.

Relax and enjoy the chance to doodle and experiment. At this stage it doesn't matter what it looks like – it is simply a way of clarifying your ideas. Try out several different arrangements, varying the size and position of lettering and picture. Are there too many words? Can you make it easier to read by arranging the words differently? Is the design well-balanced? Is there one dominant element to catch the eye? Now is the time to change and adapt.

Planning with coloured shapes

One of the difficulties for beginners is to stand back and get an overall view rather than getting bogged down in detail. If doodling does not come easily to you, try the following method a few times to help you loosen up and become more flexible in your approach.

Cut out, or tear, shapes from coloured paper to represent the various elements of your design – strips for lines of lettering and blobs of different sizes and colours to give a rough impression of the picture. For example, a bunch of daffodils would be made up of yellow blobs and green strips. Play around with the shapes, looking at the pattern they make on the background. Stand back or half-close your eyes to see the general effect, which is quite different from getting the detail right. See how the blocks or strips of lettering balance up with the rest of the composition.

The second stage of planning

Once you are satisfied with the layout:

1 **Decide which technique** to use for the poster itself. Will you use paint, crayon, felt pen, collage... or a mixture? Is there a quicker, simpler or more effective method than the one you first envisaged?

2 **Select your colour scheme.** Keep it simple – not too many different colours.

3 **Choose your background** paper or card and make sure the lettering will show up against it. (Try it out on the back if you're not sure).

Sketch faintly first to get the positions right.

4 **Sketch your design roughly and very faintly in pencil on the background,** scaling it up from the preliminary sketch. When you are satisfied that the letters and picture are properly positioned, you can confidently take up your pen, paintbrush or glue spreader. Any sketchy pencil marks still visible when the poster is finished can be removed with a soft rubber.

LAYOUT

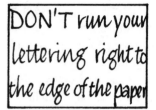

Some general hints

Leave a margin. Don't run your lettering right to the edge of the paper. The design will look more attractive if you leave some space around the edge.

Line up your lettering. It looks more professional if you pack the lettering together in imaginary 'boxes', rather than letting it straggle all over the paper. An untidy-looking poster can be improved just by giving the writing a straight margin on one side. You may also find that aligning the writing with the edge of the picture will give the poster a more finished look.

Don't be afraid of empty space. The shapes made by the spaces around the lettering and picture are part of the design. Train your eye to notice the shape of the 'negative space' as well as the positive elements in the design.

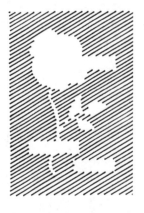

Be aware of the shape of the 'negative' space.

Line up your lettering.

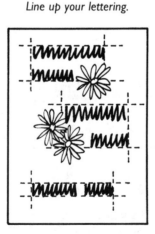

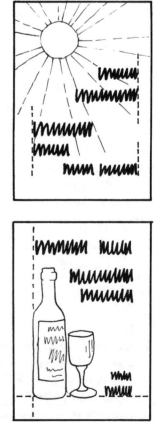

TIP **Centred lettering**

If you need centred lettering without the aid of a computer, divide the total number of letters (including spaces) in half, mark the centre of the paper and work outwards from the middle.

Components of a good layout

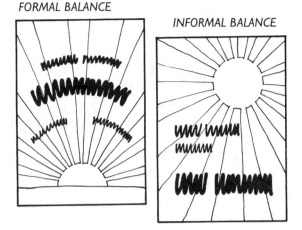

FORMAL BALANCE

INFORMAL BALANCE

Balance. This can be achieved in two ways:

1 **Formal** (symmetrical) balance is when the two sides of the design are mirror images of each other. This sort of layout is safe but unexciting – suitable, perhaps, for a formal church service or civic occasion.

2 **Informal** (asymmetrical) balance is more interesting. An area of strong or dark colour

Most of the layouts in this chapter are informal. Can you find any other formal ones?

on one side of the poster is balanced by something on the other side that appears to have an equal weight. This sort of balance needs to be sensed rather than measured.

Scale. Writing that is too small will look insignificant. Large writing can overwhelm a small picture.

Unity. The different elements can touch, overlap or lead into one another. If they appear to have no connection, it is difficult to take in all the information at one glance.

Variety. Introduce interest and emphasise important elements of the design through contrasts of size, weight and colour. Lettering that is all the same size and equally spaced will not attract attention. Words can be slanted or arched, spread or condensed to add variety.

Dominance. One element in the design should dominate, to give the eye a starting point. It should draw attention to whatever is most important – it

Elements can touch and overlap.

might be a word, a phrase or a picture. It is usually near the top or towards the centre.

To provide a focal point, the dominant element is usually larger, heavier or more brightly-coloured than the rest of the poster. The same effect can be achieved by isolating one element in an area of empty space. See next page.

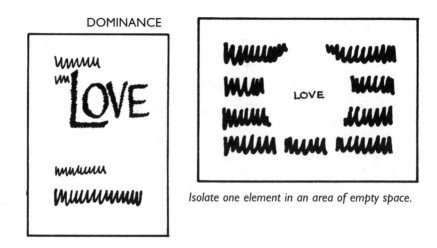

DOMINANCE

Isolate one element in an area of empty space.

PUBLICITY POSTERS

Posters advertising specific events require careful planning if they are to achieve their purpose. They can be an exciting tool for evangelism or a time-consuming chore. They may not be up very long and are unlikely to be re-used. It is therefore essential to discover methods that are effective, economical and quick.

The most common problem is too much information, which causes difficulties for both the maker and the reader. Your first job, therefore, is to prune drastically.

1 **Simplify,** cutting out anything superfluous, re-wording where appropriate, but making sure you retain the essentials. If necessary, give a contact phone number for further details. Phrases like 'You are very welcome' or 'Please come' can usually be left out.

2 **Organise the words into groups,** checking that you have answered the obvious questions:
   What is the event?
   When?
   What time?
   Where?
You may be able to leave out 'where' if the poster is going up at the place where the event will be held.

3 **List the items in order of priority.** Usually it is the title or description of the event which will provide the focus (eg *YOUTH CLUB SOCCER MATCH'* or *'SPECIAL FAMILY SERVICE')*. You might decide instead to give prominence to the speaker's name (*'BILLY GRAHAM VIDEO')* or the day (*'EASTER DAY Celebration')* or the place (*'Fireworks at ELIZABETH CASTLE')*. By deciding the order before you start, you will avoid emphasising unimportant details.

The title or theme of the event may give you an idea for a picture.

4 **Create visual interest.** The most satisfying part of the whole operation is to find a way of bringing the poster to life. If you can, use a picture to draw attention to the most important item of information. If the main heading you have been given is too general to give you a lead – eg *'Women's Meeting'* or *'Bible Convention'* – find out if the organiser has a particular theme in mind or, better still, an interesting-sounding title. *'Fun with Flowers'* or *'The Stone the Builders Rejected'* or *'Running the Race'* would offer more scope for the imagination than the titles mentioned above.

If, because of limited information, you cannot find a way of portraying the main purpose of the event pictorially, you may have to resort to a steaming cup of coffee or a group of people enjoying themselves.

Where no picture seems appropriate, think of another way of creating interest. Use unusual colours, strong contrasts or one huge word or initial letter to draw the viewer into the poster. Remember, though, that however exciting your poster may look, it will not achieve its purpose unless it is easy to read.

5 **Choose an appropriate style.** Use a colour scheme and lettering that are in keeping with the event you are advertising. Torn diagonal strips of fluorescent paper might be just right for a concert of loud electronic music aimed at teenagers. Nostalgic images and a gentle colour scheme would be more suitable for the elderly ladies' tea and talk. If your poster is aimed at men, look for an element of humour and avoid sentimentality. If your target is the mums and toddlers group, try bright primary colours and simple lettering.

The poster should give a hint of what type of event to expect. It is no good raising false expectations for a mundane planning meeting. However, a big evangelistic rally deserves stimulating and imaginative publicity.

6 **Link with other publicity items.** If you intend to advertise your event by means of invitation cards, leaflets, car stickers, T-shirts, helium balloons or a banner over the church door, it is a good idea to stick to the same design and colour throughout. People are used to recognising a product or an organisation by its logo, typeface and colour scheme. Repetition of a strong image and an interesting title will ensure that your church event does not pass unnoticed.

7 **Use an informal layout.** It saves time (unless you are using a computer) and it looks more interesting. The quickest way is to run most of the information from a straight margin on the left-hand side, and balance this with one or two chunks of writing, and/or a picture, on the right.

A straight margin on the left is easiest.

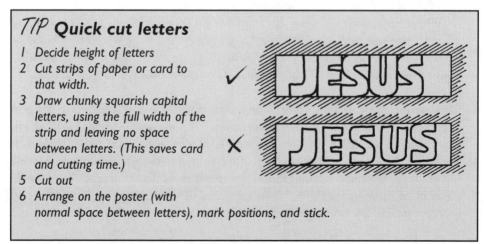

TIP Quick cut letters

1 Decide height of letters
2 Cut strips of paper or card to that width.
3 Draw chunky squarish capital letters, using the full width of the strip and leaving no space between letters. (This saves card and cutting time.)
5 Cut out
6 Arrange on the poster (with normal space between letters), mark positions, and stick.

8 **Look for short cuts.** Will it be quicker and more effective to do the lettering by hand, or to use a computer, dry transfer or stencils? See pages 77-81 (*The Lettering*).

If the church has had invitation cards printed, use a photocopier to enlarge selected bits of information for your poster. Cut up, rearrange and add colour for maximum impact. If you are given a small, dull, printed poster to put on the notice-board, you will need to find ways of making it more eye-catching. See pages 143-146 (*Display*) for some suggestions.

9 **Rule guide-lines** if you are doing the lettering by hand. It is tempting not to bother, but well worth the time it takes. A drawing board with parallel motion makes the job easy. Failing that, either a do-it-yourself drawing board with a T-square, or a 'rolling ruler', would be a sound investment. See pages 122-123 (*Materials*).

If you have to work with an ordinary ruler on the kitchen table, here are some hints to save you wasting too much time:

a Before ruling any lines, sketch out the writing very faintly and roughly on the actual poster to get an idea of size and spacing.

b If it happens that you need lettering about 3cm high (ie the width of your ruler) simply draw a line along both the top and bottom of the ruler to provide your guide-lines.

c To mark the top and bottom of all other sizes of writing, a transparent plastic ruler is best. Having ruled your base line, you can use the markings on the ruler to check that the second line is parallel to the first.

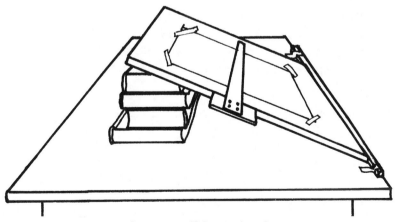

Do-it -yourself drawing board.

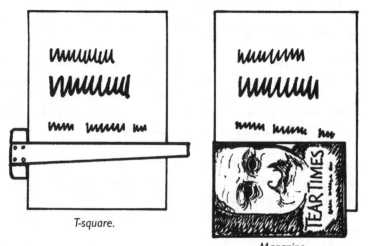

T-square.

Magazine.

d   If you do not have a T-square, use the corner of a book, a magazine or another sheet of paper to check that your lines are at right angles to the edge of the paper. It is irritating to find, after finishing a poster, that all the lines of writing slope downhill.

e   Rule all your lines faintly with a soft pencil so that you can rub them out afterwards (making sure the ink is dry first!)

TRY THIS EXERCISE

If you were given the following information and asked to make a poster to put up outside the church, how would you go about it? Find some paper now and sketch out a few ideas, remembering to cut out all non-essential details.

On Sunday October 12th, St Matthew's will be having the first of its new-style family services at 10.30 am. The children will join us in worship till 11 o'clock and then go out to group activities in the hall. The morning service will follow this pattern each week until Christmas when we will review the situation.

You will find two possible solutions at the end of this chapter.

CORRECTING MISTAKES

Even the most careful planning will not eliminate mistakes altogether. Resist the impulse to tear up your work and start again, or to put it on one side and forget about it. If your poster is going to be seen from a distance, displayed behind glass or photocopied before being put up, corrections are unlikely to be noticed. Often you can simply paint over the error or stick a piece of paper over it, or erase it with an ink rubber (or an ordinary rubber after damping the paper).

There are times when it is wise to leave small errors alone rather than draw attention to them with an ugly correction. People often read what they expect to see rather than what is actually there. At a recent exhibition in our church, one of the posters was a watercolour painting of dandelion flowers and seed heads being blown by the wind, with the words 'Breath on me, breath of God'. It was surprising how many people commented on the poster without noticing the spelling mistake. (Did you notice?)

If you feel it is important to do an almost invisible correction, this is the way to go about it:

1 Place a piece of paper, the same as that used for the poster, directly underneath the error.
2 Using a scalpel or craft knife, cut round the mistake, cutting through both layers of paper at once.
3 You will now have a hole and a replacement patch exactly the same size. Turn the poster over and stick the patch in place, using sticky tape on the reverse side.
4 Turn back to the right side and correct the error.

COLOUR

Use colour strategically

It is not necessary or desirable to use a whole palette of colours on every poster. A bold design in black and white, with one strategically placed area of colour, is more dramatic than a muddle of different colours without a plan. Areas of colour should be solid and chunky. Remember that thin lines have no impact.

Collect colour schemes

There is no copyright on colour schemes, so keep your eyes open and glean ideas from other people.

Notice the difference between **harmony** and **contrast.** A harmonious colour scheme (often used for soft furnishings) uses colours that blend well. Harmony appeals, soothes and comforts. Contrasting colours, such as the 'complementary colours' – red and green, yellow and violet or blue and orange – can be exciting or disturbing.

Whether you choose a contrasting or a harmonious colour scheme, tonal contrast (ie light and dark) is always important. Not only does it add impact to the design, but it is necessary in order to make the words easy to read. Black-and-white gives the strongest tonal contrast but there are many other possibilities. Try dark green on pale yellow, silver on navy blue, violet on peach... Experiment and see which colours show up best.

A poster composed entirely of bright colours will be less effective than one where they are set against a neutral background. Black, white, cream, and dark brown are useful as a foil, to make bright colours seem even brighter by comparison. Bear in mind that the amount of colour used, and the position where it is placed, will affect the way the poster works. A small area of sharply contrasting colour draws the eye to that spot.

Colours convey a mood

Colours have particular associations in our minds. We talk about 'seeing red' or 'feeling blue'. Certain colours evoke seasons of the year (such as brown and orange for autumn), or festivals (red and green for Christmas).

We talk of warm colours (red, orange and yellow) and cool colours (blue and violet). Red is an exciting colour which seems to reach out and grab you. It is associated with blood and fire. Blue, the colour of the sky, is more peaceful – it tends

Exercise on page 94.

to recede into the background. Yellow reminds us of brightness and sunshine. Green is the colour of life and growth.

While some colour associations are general, others are specific to a certain place or group of people – the colours of the local football team, for instance, or the national flag. Be aware that other people might not react to certain colours in the way you do. In Britain, white is used for weddings. In India it is used for funerals. Another example is the tradition that white represents good and black evil, which for black people may be deeply offensive.

> ## FIVE MAIN ELEMENTS OF POSTER DESIGN
> **1 Colour**
> **2 Contrast**
> **3 Balance**
> **4 Simplicity**
> **5 Freshness**

Use colour to reinforce the message

Make colour work for you. The colours you choose should reinforce the message of the poster. With an infinite number of possible colour combinations to choose from, we can all find different ways of creating interesting posters. A little time spent considering which colours to use, and trying different combinations, can make a huge difference to the effectiveness of each poster.

> ### TRY THIS EXERCISE
> Spend a few minutes now thinking what colour schemes might be suitable for
> * a spring flower festival
> * a talk about missionary work in Uganda
> * a firework party
> * a day of prayer for the victims of a local tragedy.

Exercise on page 104.

11 Materials

You don't need expensive equipment to start making posters. Enlist the help of other church members and many of the basic essentials can be found stored away in desk drawers, garages and lofts.

Gradually you will become aware of items you would like to buy to make the job easier and the results more effective. Your church may already see this as a legitimate part of its budget. If not, until other people see the need for posters, a few materials will need to be bought by the poster-makers themselves.

IF YOUR BUDGET IS TIGHT

Scrap paper for trying out ideas is the first thing you need. The only other requirements at planning stage are a pencil and a rubber.

A large sheet of paper or card will be needed for the actual poster. Buying a pristine sheet of coloured card from the stationer may give you great satisfaction, but it is not essential. Excellent results can be achieved using plain wallpaper, shelf paper or the backs of old posters.

Pen, paint or glue (depending on how you intend to proceed) will be next on the list. These you will probably have to buy, but take care if money is short, because buying the cheapest item on the market may be false economy.

Avoid those attractive packs of cheap fibre-tip pens with thirty or more colours. The points are too fine and the colours too weak to make an impact. It is better to spend the money on one thick, black marker with permanent ink which will last well (provided you replace the cap) and will not fade. Alternatively, experiment with some of the do-it-yourself options described on page 115.

The second item to avoid is a cheap paint-box, which will only cause frustration, with wishy-washy colours and a brush that moults. Powder paint and colour blocks, described on page 116, are economical and practical for posters. Leftovers of household emulsion paint can be used straight from the can if the colour is suitable, or powder paint can be mixed in to produce the colour you want.

For bold strokes of colour the cheapest brushes are hog (bristle). For fine detail you will need a nylon brush, which is slightly more expensive. For filling in large areas of background colour you could use a house painting brush or even a paint roller. Alternatively, try applying paint with a sponge, a swab of cotton wool or any of the other methods described on pages 57-63 (*The Picture*). These are fun as well as producing interesting results.

If you want to experiment with colour but don't feel very confident about using paint, buy a small box of oil pastels instead. They are inexpensive, versatile and easy to use.

Glue sticks, while convenient to use, are not economical for large-scale poster work. Flour-and-water paste is a useful stand-by – a tablespoon of flour mixed with a little water to a thick paste will stick ordinary paper and card, though not shiny materials. Wallpaper paste is also cheap, and a little goes a long way. Check whether it contains fungicide, which can cause skin irritation. If this is a problem, try 'Scola Cell', designed for use in schools and playgroups.

If you don't have a glue spreader or brush, a small piece of card or folded paper will serve the purpose.

Using scrap materials

Make the most of limited resources by putting to good use materials that other people have discarded.

If you have worked with young children, you will know that cardboard tubes, egg boxes, paint, play dough and dressing up clothes provide hours of imaginative play, while sophisticated, battery-operated toys are often laid aside within minutes.

In a similar way, the poster-maker presented with a varied selection of scrap materials can be inspired by the nature of the materials themselves. Twigs, straw, wood shavings, feathers and sequins each bring to mind associated ideas. Feathers remind us of birds, but also of lightness and perhaps frivolity; twigs might convey the idea of brittleness or new growth. We may choose to bring out the obvious connection (wood shavings and carpentry, for instance) or something different suggested by the shape, texture or colour of the object (such as using wood shavings as hair).

Recycling 'junk' is not simply a way of saving money or reducing pressure on the waste disposal system. It provides a stimulus for novel ideas. So start collecting!

If you are a naturally tidy person, you are probably horrified at the thought of trying to store all this rubbish. There is a balance to be struck. The clinically neat cupboard with few materials tends to discourage creativity. On the other hand, a collection of scrap materials can quickly degenerate into a mess of crumpled paper,

SCRAP MATERIALS

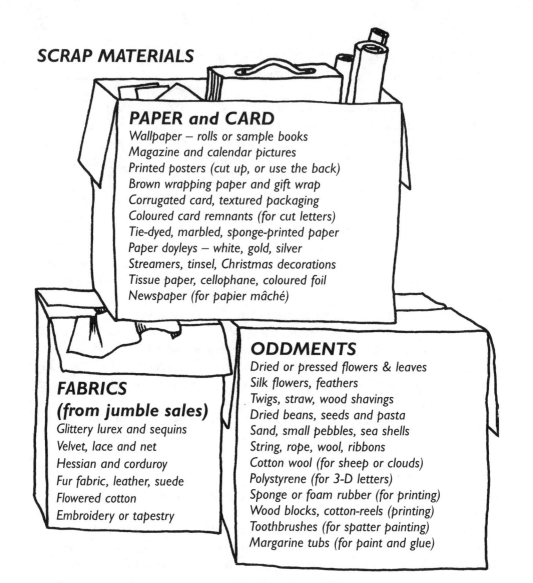

PAPER and CARD
Wallpaper – rolls or sample books
Magazine and calendar pictures
Printed posters (cut up, or use the back)
Brown wrapping paper and gift wrap
Corrugated card, textured packaging
Coloured card remnants (for cut letters)
Tie-dyed, marbled, sponge-printed paper
Paper doyleys – white, gold, silver
Streamers, tinsel, Christmas decorations
Tissue paper, cellophane, coloured foil
Newspaper (for papier mâché)

**FABRICS
(from jumble sales)**
Glittery lurex and sequins
Velvet, lace and net
Hessian and corduroy
Fur fabric, leather, suede
Flowered cotton
Embroidery or tapestry

ODDMENTS
Dried or pressed flowers & leaves
Silk flowers, feathers
Twigs, straw, wood shavings
Dried beans, seeds and pasta
Sand, small pebbles, sea shells
String, rope, wool, ribbons
Cotton wool (for sheep or clouds)
Polystyrene (for 3-D letters)
Sponge or foam rubber (for printing)
Wood blocks, cotton-reels (printing)
Toothbrushes (for spatter painting)
Margarine tubs (for paint and glue)

musty fabrics and tatty oddments which no-one wants to use. To facilitate imaginative poster-making, you will need clearly labelled boxes and a regular sort-out.

MATERIALS AND EQUIPMENT TO BUY

If your church recognises the importance of posters and has agreed a budget to cover expenses, what should you buy?

Factors to take into account:

- How much money is available
- Time and energy involved in frequent shopping trips
- Whether materials are available locally or need to be bought by mail order or by someone travelling away from home
- Space available for storage
- Size, position and weather resistance of the display board
- Preferences of existing poster-makers
- How many people are likely to be making posters at one time.

Storage space and money permitting, the widest possible choice of materials should be provided, to encourage variety and inventiveness. Avoid outlay on expensive and specialised equipment until you are sure it is necessary.

A list of mail order suppliers can be found on page 153.

PAPER

Look around to see what papers are readily available, then experiment to find the most practical and economical for your purposes.

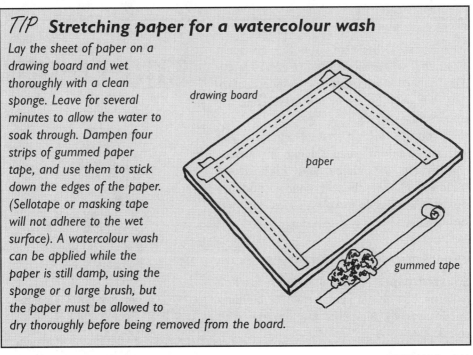

TIP **Stretching paper for a watercolour wash**

Lay the sheet of paper on a drawing board and wet thoroughly with a clean sponge. Leave for several minutes to allow the water to soak through. Dampen four strips of gummed paper tape, and use them to stick down the edges of the paper. (Sellotape or masking tape will not adhere to the wet surface). A watercolour wash can be applied while the paper is still damp, using the sponge or a large brush, but the paper must be allowed to dry thoroughly before being removed from the board.

drawing board

paper

gummed tape

What size? Measure the display board before buying paper. If you buy the right size, you will not waste time trimming edges or sticking sheets together.

What method? Choose thick paper or card if you are using water-based paint, to minimise puckering when wet. (To ensure a perfectly flat poster, you might need to pre-stretch the paper – see TIP below). A glossy surface may reject the paint (unless you use acrylic, oil or domestic gloss paint). Pastels work best on textured paper, whereas for calligraphy a smooth surface is preferable.

What sort of display? For pasting up, thin paper such as frieze paper is suitable. (It is sold by the roll in bright colours, white on the back). If you are using pins and hope to re-use the poster, you will need something more durable.

What colour? White and black are good backgrounds for bright lettering or pictures, but if you are buying for a group, offer as wide a range of background colours as possible.

What price? Sometimes you will need to spend more to get exactly the right colour or texture, or you may need thick board for a poster that will be re-used over and

---

TIP **Test paper for fading**

Cut two strips from the edge of a sheet of paper. Leave one on a sunny windowsill and protect the other by placing inside a book. After a couple of weeks, compare the two.

---

over again. Otherwise, buy the cheapest paper that will achieve the effect you want. 'Play paper' is adequate for indoor posters that will only be up a few days, but the colours fade quickly.

If you are making posters regularly, you will not want to keep paying the prices charged in art shops and high street stationers. For a cheaper source, find out where local schools and playgroups buy their supplies.

Papers for special purposes

Squared paper – for imitating cross-stitch patterns, like an old sampler, or for building up designs by filling in the squares with colour

Imitating cross-stitch patterns.

Crêpe paper – for flower petals and leaves

Coloured corrugated card – to add texture

Fluorescent paper, foil, holographic paper and cellophane – for special effects.

Coloured adhesive labels – for quick cut-out letters

Stars (gold and silver)

Tracing paper (or kitchen greaseproof paper, which is cheaper).

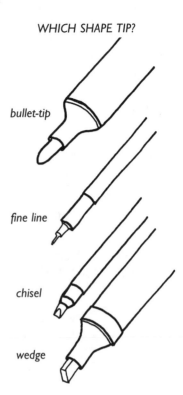

WHICH SHAPE TIP?

bullet-tip

fine line

chisel

wedge

PENS

Marker pens

The choice may seem bewildering, but there are basically three decisions to make:

- Which type of ink: spirit-based or water-based?
- Which shape tip: bullet, chisel or fine line?
- Which colour?

Which ink? Spirit-based markers are best for posters since they give a strong, permanent colour which is waterproof and does not fade. Also they can be used on shiny or greasy surfaces, such as plastic, foil or over oil pastels. Permanent markers should be used in a well-ventilated room and care must be taken not to get marks on clothes and furniture.

Which tip? The choice of tip will depend on how you intend to use it. A bullet-tip is generally the most useful for drawing and informal lettering. Berol's 'Toughpoint' is a good, hard-wearing example.

Chisel- or wedge-shaped tips can be used to produce thick and thin strokes for calligraphy. Some people find this technique easy to master, while others struggle without success. If you find it difficult, use a bullet-tip pen and find other ways of writing that suit you better.

A fine point is needed for small lettering and detail. Broad-tipped markers can be used for filling in areas of solid colour but it is cheaper and more effective to use paint or oil pastels.

Which colour? Black is essential, for outlines and for clear, easy-to-read writing. Red, blue and green add variety. Yellow is less useful – it does not show up well against a white background, and on a dark background yellow marker ink disappears altogether.

If you want to write on a dark background, look for paint markers, which contain opaque paint rather than ink. White and yellow make a good contrast on black. Shake the pen well to mix up the paint, and press up and down on the point several times to get it started.

Metallic markers are similar, containing opaque silver or gold paint which shows

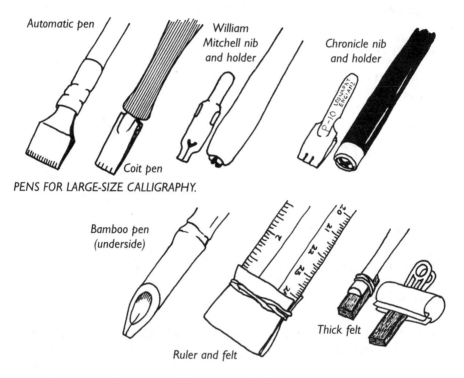

PENS FOR LARGE-SIZE CALLIGRAPHY.

up particularly well on black. They are available in thicknesses from broad to extra fine and can make a simple poster look special.

Calligraphy pens

If you have already mastered the art of small-size calligraphy, and want to use the skill for posters, you may have had difficulty finding a suitably large pen. Here are some suggestions:

Chisel-edge markers (sometimes sold as 'calligraphy pens') are easy to use but do not give the crisp definition of a metal nib, especially once the edge gets fuzzy with age. You may be able to lengthen the life of a felt-tip by trimming the end with a craft knife.

'Automatic' or 'Coit' pens are the best for large size calligraphy. Both have a broad metal nib with a special reservoir that can be filled with ink or paint. They are available in a variety of sizes from 1.5mm to 38mm. The problem is that you are unlikely to find them except in a specialist shop. A list of mail order suppliers can be found on page 153.

'Chronicle' poster nibs (sizes 4mm to 15mm), produced by the Manuscript Pen Company, are another option. (Address page 153).

Two pencils or fine-tip pens to give an outline.

Mitchell's poster nibs are easier to find in non-specialist shops, but they are not available in such large sizes.

Do-it-yourself options include cutting your own pen from bamboo (or use balsa wood or a lolly-stick). For really large letters, a strip of thin felt can be tied over the end of a ruler, or thick felt can be attached to a stick or held in a bulldog clip.

Two pencils or fine-tip pens, fastened together tightly with rubber bands, can be used to provide an outline, which is then shaded or coloured in.

A photocopier can be used to enlarge small size calligraphy.

ADHESIVES

PVA adhesive is the most generally useful for posters – a thick white liquid which dries fairly quickly to a transparent, flexible film (or blob). It is easily applied, either straight from the nozzle of the container, or using a plastic spreader, a brush or a small piece of cardboard. It can be diluted with water for a thinner consistency or if it becomes too thick after long storage. Mixed with powder paint, it can be applied thickly, to give texture to the paint, or 'piped' onto the paper through a nozzle, like icing on a cake.

There are two sorts of PVA adhesive. The washable version, sold under brand names such as School Glue or Kids' Glue, can be washed out of clothes and brushes even after it has dried. The non-washable type, such as Marvin Medium, is stronger and more versatile, but brushes will be ruined if it is allowed to dry on them.

Rubber-based adhesives such as Copydex, are similar to PVA but not water-soluble. They are not ideal for posters you hope to re-use, since they become yellow with age and can leave unsightly marks.

Solid glue sticks, like Pritt, are useful for fiddly or temporary jobs, like assembling clip art for photocopying. But the glue is not strong enough for collage (you are liable to find bits falling off your poster afterwards).

A tube of impact adhesive, which is strong and quick-drying, may sometimes be needed to attach heavy or awkwardly-shaped items.

Aerosol sprays are convenient to use with thin papers, like tissue paper, which tear easily and are liable to stretch and wrinkle, and also for the slippery, clingy type of metallic gift-wrap. However, spray adhesive should be avoided where possible. Apart from long-term damage to the environment, there are more immediate problems. The tiny particles floating in the air are liable to be breathed into the lungs, as well as landing on furniture where they attract dust.

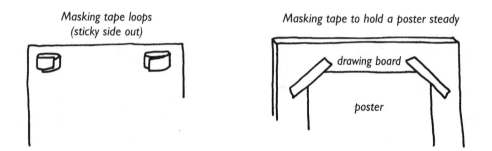

Masking tape loops
(sticky side out)

Masking tape to hold a poster steady

drawing board

poster

Blu-tack or small loops of masking tape can be used for temporary fixing, such as when a panel of information needs to be updated each week. Both are 'low tack', which means they can be removed from most surfaces without leaving a mark. Masking tape is also useful for holding a poster steady on a drawing board while you are working on it.

Double-sided sticky tape is convenient for sticking up posters but a nuisance when storing them. After use, cover the sticky tape with strips of paper to avoid damage to other posters.

PAINT

Blocks of solid poster colour are cheap, convenient and easy to store, but you have to work quite hard to produce a strong colour.

Jars or tubs (with paint the consistency of jam) are a little more expensive, but have the advantage that you can lay the paint on thickly if you want to.

Powder paint is cheapest and worth considering if you are going to use a lot of paint. The disadvantage is that

> *TIP* **Use clean paint water**
> Change the water frequently or use several jars, especially for white or yellow paint, to avoid spoiling the clarity of your poster.

you have to mix it up yourself with water or, for a better consistency, with wallpaper paste, PVA adhesive or household emulsion paint.

Ready-mix is a useful alternative – a thick liquid sold in containers like washing-up liquid bottles.

Designers' Gouache is the best paint for most poster work. It is sold in tubes and can be diluted with water. The colours are intense, opaque and have good covering power, even on tinted paper, allowing areas of consistent flat colour to be laid down. It is not necessary to buy a big range. Start with a few basic colours (eg red, yellow, blue, black, white) and add others as you need them.

Acrylic paint also comes in tubes and is similar in application, though it does not have quite the covering power of gouache. Its major advantage is that, once dry, the paint is completely waterproof. It can be used on glossy and even greasy surfaces (to which other water-based paints will not adhere) and on paper which will be rolled for storage, since it neither cracks nor peels. Acrylic paint is water-soluble when wet, but care must be taken not to allow it to dry on the brush. When dry, acrylics have a slightly shiny appearance, whereas gouache dries matt.

Plaka (made by Pelikan and sold in jars) is also good for posters, having good covering power and being water-soluble when wet but light-fast and water resistant once dry.

Watercolour paint is transparent, rather than opaque, which means that mistakes cannot be covered up, as they can with acrylics, by simply painting over them. The luminous quality of watercolour makes it ideal for background washes of sky, sea or soft landscapes, onto which the lettering can be superimposed using a different medium. A few drops of gum arabic (from an art shop), added to the paint, will prevent it being rubbed away when erasing pencil lines.

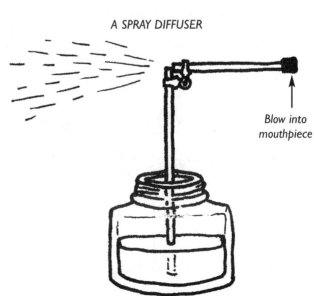

A SPRAY DIFFUSER

Blow into mouthpiece

Masking fluid, a rubber solution which, again, is obtainable in art shops, produces interesting effects in conjunction with watercolour. See page 59 (*The Picture*).

Spray paint cans are convenient and fun to use. See page 61 (*The Picture*). However, they are not cheap and where there is an alternative, they should be avoided for the same reasons as spray adhesives.

A spray diffuser or a garden or cosmetic spray bottle filled with ink or paint can be used instead.

BRUSHES

If you are likely to do much painting, it is worth buying a few of the best brushes you can afford. Look after them well and they will last a lifetime.

What type?

Bristle is cheap, and useful for applying paint thickly.

BRUSH SHAPES

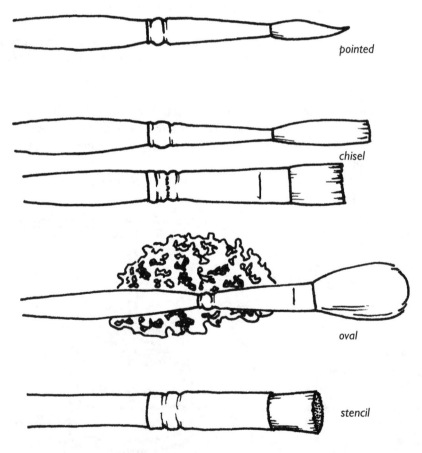

pointed

chisel

oval

stencil

Hair (real or artificial) is suitable for any water-based paint. The best and most expensive are sable, which is responsive and supple, as well as tapering to a fine point. Nylon and other synthetic fibres are more reasonably priced.

Any brush can be used with poster paint or gouache, which wash out easily, but don't risk using an expensive brush for acrylics.

What shape?

Pointed brushes are the most useful. Two or three brushes of this shape in different sizes should cover most purposes.

Chisel-edge lettering brushes have hair of equal length cut square at the end, rather than tapering to a point. They may be made of hair, bristle or synthetic fibre. The longer the hair the more paint the brush will hold, but beginners will find a short or medium length easier to control.

Oval-shaped full brushes are good for laying down washes but a sponge will do.

Flat-ended stiff stencil brushes are used only for stencilling. They are held upright and the paint is applied with a dabbing motion.

PASTELS AND CRAYONS

Oil pastels are a cheap and convenient alternative to paint, invaluable for quick filling in of outline letters when a poster is needed in a hurry. There are three ways of applying them:

- Firm pressure gives areas of solid bright colour.
- Light strokes can be used for subtle shading (especially effective on textured paper). When using different colours together avoid overworking – it produces a muddy result.
- A paint-like effect can be achieved by applying white spirit or turpentine with a brush after the colour has been laid down on the paper.

Oil pastels do not smudge as easily as soft pastels, and because they are waterproof they are useful for outdoor display.

Soft pastels, because of their high proportion of pigment, offer a unique richness of colour. Whereas, with paint, endless variations can be mixed from a small selection of colours, with pastels it is

> *TIP* **Tinting paper**
>
> *Small pieces of broken pastel need not be wasted — they can be used to add interest to a sheet of plain paper. Grind the broken pastel finely. Dab a damp cloth or sponge on to the colour, and either spread it evenly over the whole surface or create a mottled pattern.*

good to start with a wide range of colours because blending is done on the paper itself.

Soft pastels need a textured paper which provides a tooth to hold the particles. Firm, light strokes should be used so that other colours can be added afterwards without clogging the grain of the paper. If you are not happy with the result, dust off the excess with cotton wool or a bristle brush, and try again. Gentle smudging with the finger produces soft misty effects.

> ## *TIP* **Spraying fixative**
> *Rather than an aerosol can, consider buying a bottle of fixative and a spray diffuser. Lay the drawing flat and blow the spray over it.*

Unintentional smudging is the main problem with soft pastels. The finished poster needs to be protected immediately by spraying with fixative.

Charcoal is ideal for bold, spontaneous drawings. Lines and shading vary from pale grey to intense black. Like pastels, charcoal works best on textured rather than smooth paper.

The disadvantages are that it is messy and brittle and needs immediate fixing. To avoid smudging as you work, draw with your hand raised off the paper.

Crayons come in various forms, but strictly speaking the term does not include coloured pencils, though that is what many people mean when they use the word 'crayon'.

> **Wax crayons** are cheap, clean and non-toxic, but don't assume that they are only for children. They are fun to use and can encourage an informal, experimental approach. Use them to bring a light touch to a poster for a church outing or family fun day. Wax crayons are particularly useful for rubbings and wax-resist. See page 59 (*The Picture*).

> **Square-section Conté crayons** are now produced in a wide range of colours, but you could limit yourself to the original natural colours – black, white, bistre (brown) and sanguine (reddish-brown) – to make a change from bright primary colours. Try imitating the effect of light and shade on a ploughed field, or highlights on a head of hair.

> **Water-soluble crayons,** such as those produced by Caran d'Ache, can be used in a variety of ways. Watercolour effects can be achieved either by adding water with a fine brush to a small area of the crayon drawing at a time, or by brushing over the whole area, leaving a vague impression of the original drawing.

CUTTING TOOLS

Scissors. Whatever else you decide to do without, buy one good pair of scissors, (preferably with sharp points for cutting out the middles of letters), and use them only for paper and card.

A craft knife with a sharp point, or a scalpel, will be needed for some intricate jobs. Keep a protective cover over the blade when not in use (a sheath made of card and Sellotape will do) and store out of reach of children. The cheap, plastic-handled, disposable type of knife is fine for most purposes.

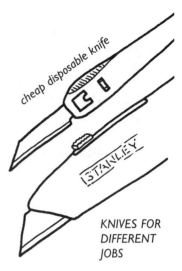

KNIVES FOR DIFFERENT JOBS

A 'Stanley' knife with a broad, solid blade is useful for cutting thick card and tough craft materials. When cutting straight lines, always rest

---

TIP **Quick method for trimming poster paper**

When cutting paper off a roll or trimming a sheet that is too large, you need to make sure that corners are square and sides straight. Bear in mind that
- paper naturally folds in straight lines
- machine-cut paper already has straight edges and right angled corners

1 Mark on one edge of the paper, with a pencil or your thumb nail, the place where you will start cutting

2 Fold the paper over at that point, lining up the paper edges exactly to get a right angle

3 Still holding those edges together, press the fold right across the paper

4 Unfold and cut along the fold line

This method is fairly accurate unless you are trimming a very narrow strip. In that case, check that the fold runs parallel to the edge, either by eye or by measuring at both ends.

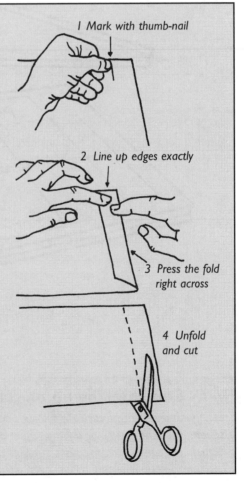

1 Mark with thumb-nail

2 Line up edges exactly

3 Press the fold right across

4 Unfold and cut

---

the blade against the edge of a ruler, preferably a metal one. Don't apply too heavy pressure at the first cut, in case the knife slips. Establish a groove in the right place and use repeated light strokes till you have cut right through.

A non-slip, self-seal cutting mat would be the best way of protecting your work surface, but a pad of newspaper will do.

A guillotine is handy for cutting large quantities of paper neatly and accurately but for a single large poster it is just as quick to rule a pencil line and use scissors.

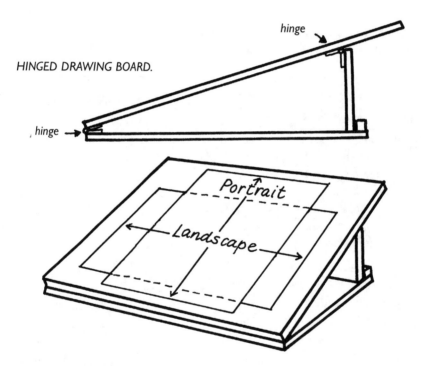

HINGED DRAWING BOARD.

TIP **Straightening up an odd-shaped piece of paper**
Start with one straight edge (by folding and cutting). If you don't have a ruler or a set square, use a magazine or another sheet of paper as a guide, to make sure the corners are square and the sides straight.

DRAWING BOARD AND T-SQUARE

A sloping drawing board will help prevent back strain caused by stooping over a table. For occasional posters it is not necessary to spend a lot of money on one with parallel motion (a system for ruling parallel lines without measuring).

As long as the surface is flat and smooth and the size right, any piece of block-board, plywood, discarded kitchen work-top or even hardboard will do. Rest the board on your lap against the table or prop it on some books (or bricks, wrapped in paper to avoid scratching the table). A piece of dowel, or a ruler, taped to the edge of the table will stop the board slipping off. See page 103 (*Planning*). A more permanent version can be made with two pieces of board hinged together. If you decide to do this, make sure the top board will be big enough to accommodate paper in either portrait or landscape position.

Parallel lines to help keep lettering regular

Rolling ruler

A T-square enables you to rule horizontal lines for lettering. For this to work properly, the left-hand edge of the board must be absolutely straight.

A set-square (triangle) resting on the T-square provides the vertical lines.

DRAWING AND LETTERING AIDS

Rulers

An ordinary ruler is one of the first things you need to buy. The transparent plastic ones are best – it is easier to judge the correct position for the line you are ruling if you can see what is underneath the ruler. The standard 30 cm (12 inch) length will do, but a longer ruler is an advantage if you are making large posters.

TIP **Ruling lines in ink**

Remember to turn over the ruler when using ink. The bevelled edge prevents ink spreading under the ruler and makes smudging less likely.

If you are using a set square or a stencil which does not have a bevelled edge, stick a strip of masking tape under the edge to raise it slightly off the paper.

Some transparent rulers have a series of parallel lines along the middle. These are helpful when ruling guide-lines for lettering, enabling you to check that your lines are parallel, and to repeat same-size lettering without complicated measuring.

A rolling ruler, if you can find one, is even more useful, especially when a lot of writing needs to be presented clearly and legibly. It incorporates a cylinder with rubber wheels, to keep lines parallel and measure the distance between them. It also has features which enable you to draw circles, measure angles and draw vertical parallel lines.

A steel ruler is an optional extra you will only need if you frequently cut thick card.

Compasses

These are useful for drawing circles, though not essential. It is usually possible to find a jar, tin, saucer or roll of sticky tape to draw round for small circles. For large circles, a piece of string tied to a drawing pin at one end and pencil at the other will serve the purpose.

Flexible curve

This is a strip of soft metal encased in vinyl, which is used like a ruler except that it makes curves instead of straight lines. It can be bent to whatever shape you require and is useful for standardising those tricky letters like S and C.

Dry transfer lettering

Small packs are widely available, but the letters are too small for most posters, and need to be enlarged on the photocopier. (The letters retain their clarity even when enlarged several times.) These small packs are good value but offer little variety. 'Letraset' and 'Chartpak' produce a wide range of typefaces, sizes, weights and colours but their sheets are expensive – especially the largest sizes, because there are so few letters per sheet.

Whether or not you buy a sheet of their letters, a Letraset or Chartpak catalogue is a marvellous resource book to have at home. The hundreds of sample alphabets will provide ideas and models for every occasion: historic and ultra-modern, formal and fantastic, serious and comic.

For information on how to use dry transfer letters, see page 78 (*The Lettering*).

Stencils and templates

Stencils are letter-shaped holes cut out of a sheet of plastic or card. They are readily available and easy to use but, again, the largest sizes can be expensive.

Templates (letters that you draw round) are easy to make. Choose a simple, bold alphabet, either drawn by hand, computer-generated or from a clip art book. Draw, trace or photocopy the letters onto a sheet of card and cut out. (If photocopying, check first that the card is suitable for the machine.)

Templates produce an outline letter, which can easily be filled in, using oil pastel, crayon, marker or paint. The only problem is that individual template letters are easily lost. Store them in marked envelopes or polythene bags.

BEATING THE WEATHER

An outdoor display board that offers protection from wind and rain – see page 138 (*Display*) – saves time and effort for the poster-maker, and encourages variety and inventiveness. If your board is not protected, you must either add a waterproof coating to every poster or make sure you use waterproof materials.

Waterproof coatings

1 **Laminating** is the best option, especially if the poster is completely encapsulated for all-round protection. Many print shops now offer this service. Unfortunately it is so expensive for large sizes that it is only worthwhile for special posters or ones which will be re-used many times.
2 **Transparent self-adhesive plastic** can be bought in rolls and used to cover posters, provided they are not too big. This adds considerably to the time it takes to make the poster, as well as to the expense. It gives good but not total protection, since water can still seep in gradually through the back.
3 **Colourless waterproof spray lacquer** is a simpler method but again offers no guarantee against extreme weather conditions.

Waterproof materials

If in doubt, test a small sample under the tap before embarking on the poster. The following should be safe:

1 Spirit-based (waterproof) marker pens
2 Oil pastels
3 Acrylic paint
4 Household emulsion paint (if the colour is pale, add powder paint)
5 Household gloss paint
6 Car spray paint
7 Non-washable PVA adhesive will ensure a strong bond for collage even in wet conditions
8 Photocopied posters are both waterproof and light-fast. Once the basic black and white design has been photocopied, colour can be added using oil pastels or waterproof paint.

Sagging paper

Why is it that the poster that looked so fresh and crisp when you pinned it up looks limp and sorry-for-itself a day later? When paper gets damp it is inclined to sag. If this is a problem, either pre-stretch it, as described on page 111, or use thicker paper or card.

Sun and wind

These can cause problems, as well as rain.

- Test paper and marker pens for fading. See page 112.
- Make sure the poster is firmly attached, using pins, paste or staples. If one corner comes loose in the wind, you are liable to lose the whole poster.

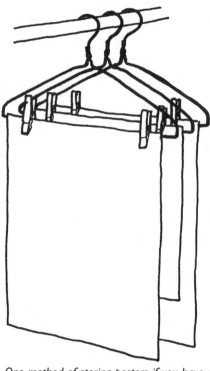

STORAGE

One method of storing posters if you have a spare wardrobe!

Finished posters are the most important and the most difficult item to store. They are best laid flat if at all possible. Shelves or drawers must be large enough to prevent damage to corners and edges. Where space is limited, posters can be stored in a carrying case or portfolio, which you can buy from an art shop or make yourself.

If you have to keep the posters at home, you may find a safe haven under the bed or, if you have small children or pets, on top of the wardrobe. Another possibility, if

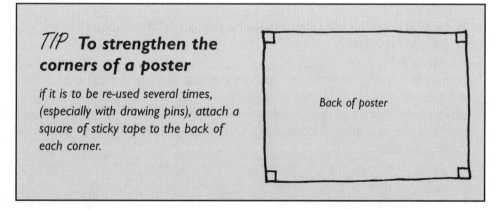

TIP **To strengthen the corners of a poster**

if it is to be re-used several times, (especially with drawing pins), attach a square of sticky tape to the back of each corner.

Back of poster

you have a spare hanging space, is to hang them from wire coat hangers, using clothes pegs or bulldog clips. If you always use thin poster paper and paint, rather than collage, you may prefer to keep the posters rolled. If so, roll them around (or inside) a cardboard tube of the correct length to prevent the paper getting flattened and crumpled.

Posters are easier to store if they are all the same size, and for this reason you may decide to stick to a standard format. But if you can allow people freedom to experiment with different sizes and shapes, you will increase the interest and enjoyment for all concerned.

Take even greater care of other people's posters than you would of your own. Until your own lovingly-made poster is damaged by someone else's carelessness, you may not realise how hurtful it can be.

Paper waiting to be used also needs special care. The appeal of a smooth, clean sheet of paper is soon lost when it begins to get creased and dog-eared. If you keep a stock of paper in various colours, spend a few minutes sorting the colours and straightening the pile, so that it is easy to see what is available, and to prevent corners getting bent because they are sticking out.

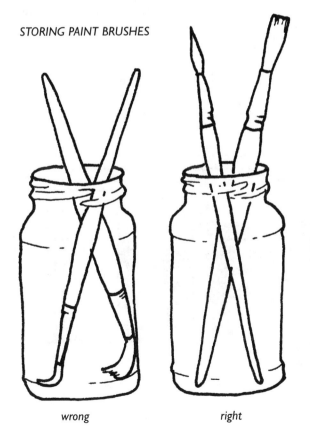

STORING PAINT BRUSHES

wrong   right

12 Display

'Wisdom calls aloud in the street,
she raises her voice in the public squares;
at the head of the noisy streets she cries out,
in the gateways of the city she makes her speech…'
Proverbs 1:20 & 21

A poster stored in a cupboard is a contradiction in terms. Until it is 'posted', (ie put up where it can be seen), it will not achieve its purpose. The Christian poster-maker cannot afford to be reticent. In order to be heard above the clamour of the world, Wisdom must raise her voice.

WHERE TO DISPLAY

The effectiveness of a poster depends to a large extent on where and how it is displayed. If your aim is to reach out to non-Christians, then posters must be put up where they will be seen. How this is done will depend on the position of the church, its age, its role in the community and its attitude to evangelism and to the arts.

A board outside the church is the most common method (see page 134), but there are other possibilities:

Windows can be used, if your church is modern with large expanses of plain glass. Stick the posters on the inside of the glass, so that they can be seen from outside. This has certain advantages over the traditional notice-board:

Transparent or mobile posters.

- **Protection.** Posters are safe from vandals and weather.
- **Convenience.** Posters can be changed while standing indoors, sheltered from cold, wind and rain.
- **Flexibility.** The position, size and shape of posters can be varied, as well as the number (one, several, or none, without giving an impression of neglect). An informal, experimental approach may seem less threatening to non-churchgoers. You could try something really unusual, like coloured cellophane that you can see right through, or a double-sided poster hanging like a mobile.
- **Attention is drawn** to the church building itself, whereas a board attached to posts or railings outside can look quite separate.

The open porch, typical of old parish churches, makes an ideal place for posters because it is available to passers-by even when the church is locked.

The inside of the church may also be suitable, especially if it is open during the week.

A church hall used by non-church groups offers scope for posters that will generate interest in the beliefs and activities of the church.

Other local churches might be glad to borrow some of your posters and this could lead to them starting a group of their own.

Shop or front-room windows, hospitals, libraries, town halls, schools, offices, doctors' surgeries are all potential sites. In fact any public building with a notice-board or big windows is worth considering. The Christian message will have more impact in a secular setting because it is unexpected; but pray and think carefully about what is appropriate for each place. *Always obtain permission before putting up posters anywhere!*

Some posters will not be suitable for showing outside the church – they may be too small, too difficult to read from a distance or the message may be more applicable to churchgoers than to people outside. If you organise a workshop for beginners or children and you are not sure what the results will be like, have an alternative, not-too-public display area in mind – in the room where work has been going on, in the church hall or Sunday School area or in the church itself. Posters need not stay up long, provided the people who have made them get a chance to see their work displayed. This is important, not only to show that what they have done is appreciated, but also so that they can see and learn from their mistakes. Children's designs can be grouped together, so that all can be seen but none assumes too great an importance. Remember that children are competitive but also sensitive.

HOW TO DISPLAY

The outside notice-board is the church's shop window and window-dressing is important. Next time you walk down your local high street, look at the shop windows and try to analyse why some make you want to go inside and buy, while others do not merit a second glance.

Some shops emphasise the cheapness of the prices, others the quality of the goods; some focus on one particular item, or a colour-coordinated range. Some seem to be saying, 'We are so confident of our reputation that we do not need to advertise'. Instead, they create a pleasurable experience which entices the customer in a subtler way. Choice of colour is important. The background is carefully designed to enhance the total impression.

There is one difference between the shop and the church. The shop window-dresser cannot be certain that the goods displayed will live up to their promise. By contrast, we need have no doubts about *him who is able to do immeasurably more than all we ask or imagine...' (Ephesians 3:20)*.

Planning

The successful window-dresser plans ahead, taking account of the seasons, local events and special promotions. The church notice-board also needs to be planned, with proper coordination between different church groups, anticipating publicity needs. Message posters can be appropriate to the seasons and church festivals, or linked to sermon themes or local news. Keeping in touch with local events requires planning that is flexible enough to accommodate changes at short notice.

Selectivity

One dress beautifully displayed is more likely to catch the eye than a window crammed with a variety of goods. In the same way, if you display one poster at a time, you focus all attention on that one poster, and increase the chances of the message reaching its target. Much of the impact will be lost when a second poster is placed alongside the first, since the two will be competing for attention. Several posters displayed at once may look bright and attractive but stand less chance of being read by the casual passer-by.

A colour scheme

Self-confident use of colour is the hallmark of the professional window-dresser. Posters also benefit from a clear colour scheme.

A white poster will not show up on a white background. If the poster and notice-board are similar in colour, lay the poster on one or more sheets of contrasting paper or card to make a border. (If you do not glue the poster to the backing, the latter can be reused.)

The colour of the backing sheet might echo the colour of the writing or pick up one of the colours in the picture. Don't introduce too many unrelated colours or the result will be a muddle. If in doubt, use black for a light-coloured poster and white for a dark one.

Choice of colour is a matter of personal taste, but don't rely on guesswork. Try different backing sheets till you find the one that brings out the best in the poster. Don't always stick to the same colours. Some posters call for dramatic contrasts, others for colours that blend harmoniously.

Experiment with unlikely combinations and you will get some pleasant surprises. Remember that the unexpected is more likely to attract attention than the predictable.

Variety

The window-dresser will try to show a representative sample of the range of merchandise sold in the shop, though not all together. Beachwear, school clothes, winter coats and party dresses will be displayed at different times. A large department store might have different windows for different types of goods – one for furniture, one for fabrics, one for china.

A thriving church may have two notice-boards: one for news of events and the other for message posters. Whether your church has one board or several, it is essential to change the display as frequently as possible. Posters are designed for immediate impact and enjoyment, rather than for their long-term aesthetic qualities, and so they should be changed quickly before people tire of them. Remember that the first sighting will be the one that counts. After that, most people will walk straight past. A variety of different posters, displayed with flair and imagination, can convey something of the energy and vitality of God the Creator.

Each poster can be displayed in any number of different ways by arranging it on backing sheets of various sizes and colours.

Here are some suggestions illustrated on pages 132 and 133:

1 **Equal border** all round (or slightly wider at the bottom).
2 **Border either side** or top and bottom.
3 **Shadow effect** – a sheet behind one corner.
4 **Opposite corners** (the same or different colours).
5 **Asymmetrical arrangements** of one or more sheets.
6 **Once-only ideas** to suit particular posters.
7 **Tilted poster** (or backing sheet).
8 **Brightly-patterned wrapping paper,** if the poster is very plain.

Try out different arrangements on the floor (or a table) indoors first, to see how they look. Even better, if you can manage it, is a piece of board the same size and colour as your notice-board.

Find your own ways of stimulating interest and introducing surprises. But aim to draw attention to the poster itself, not to the clever effects you have achieved with the backing. Remember the value of simple contrast. A plain black background often brings out the colours of the poster better than the most startling innovation you can think of.

*Equal border all round
(or slightly wider at the bottom).*

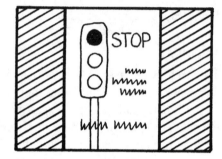

*Border either side
or top and bottom.*

*Opposite corners
(the same or different colours).*

*Shadow effect –
a sheet behind one corner.*

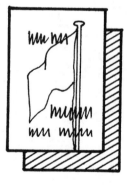

Assymetrical arrangements of one or more sheets.

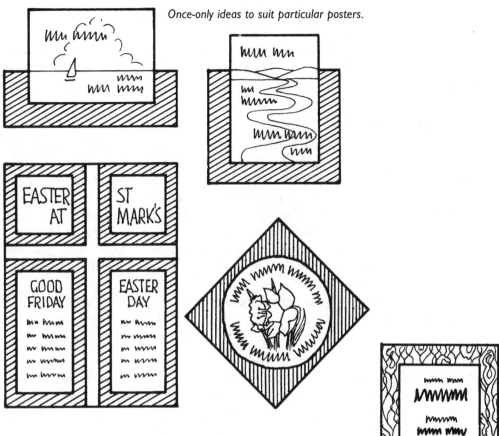

Once-only ideas to suit particular posters.

Brightly-patterned wrapping paper with a plain poster.

Tilted poster or backing sheet.

THE OUTDOOR POSTER-BOARD

If your church already has a large, weatherproof, Perspex-fronted, easy-opening poster-board, well sited where it will be seen by a large number of people, then consider yourself blessed and use it well!

Unsuitable board

If you have inherited a notice-board that is small, inconvenient, badly positioned or without weather protection, spend some time experimenting, making the best possible use of what is available, before asking your church to spend money on something that other members may consider unimportant.

Your first priority is to demonstrate that posters have a part to play in drawing in non-churchgoers, as well as in building up the faith of existing members. Secondly, you need to know exactly what you want, and why. Are you sure that a change in the size, construction or position of the board will make a significant difference to the effectiveness of the posters?

If the main problem is inconvenience when changing the posters, ask a few other people to take a turn, so that they can experience the difficulties first hand.

No board

If your church has no display-board at all, check that you have not overlooked some alternative method of displaying posters. Can you attach them to a glass door, a window or a wall? To advertise special events, could you use a portable display-board, either standing or hanging near the church door?

If none of these is suitable, and you are convinced that there is a need for a permanent poster-board outside the church, the next question is how well the board will be used. Is there someone willing to take responsibility for changing the posters regularly? A board that stands empty, or with the same poster for months on end, may be worse than none at all.

Choosing the right board

Size

The viewing distance and the speed at which people pass will determine the size of the posters. If everyone walks past close to the board, posters can be quite small. If most people will be looking from across the churchyard or from a passing car, then posters must be big, bold and simple.

If in doubt between two sizes of board, choose the larger. This allows flexibility in the method of display, and in the shapes and sizes of posters that can be used.

Position

Consider carefully before deciding on the position for the board. Choose a site passed regularly by the maximum number of people, or where a park bench or a bus

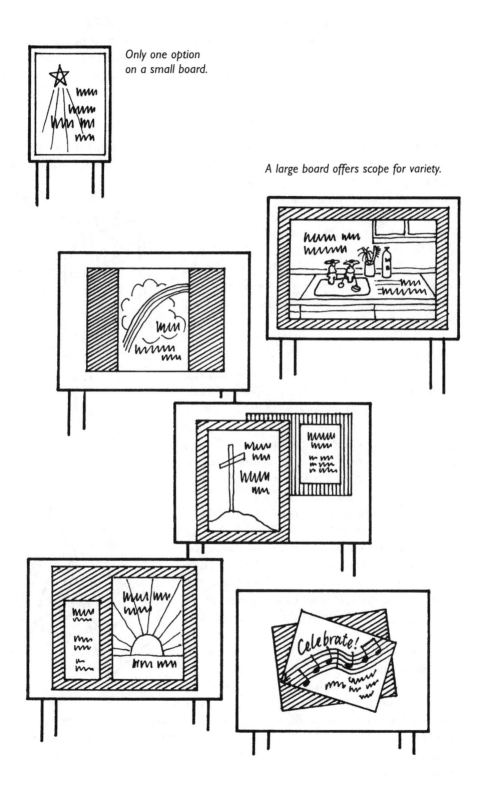

Only one option on a small board.

A large board offers scope for variety.

Celebrate!

queue provides a captive audience. Will the board be clearly visible without people having to crane their necks or go out of their way? Make sure bushes, walls or railings will not obscure the view. Should the board be parallel to the road or at an angle? Will your posters have to compete with road signs, shop displays or other posters? Will you need planning permission?

Accessibility

Make sure the board is easily accessible, to encourage regular poster changes. Having to stretch over a boundary wall or climb a ladder to put up the poster makes it tempting to leave it up 'just one more week'. In any case, the board should not be too high or too low – posters displayed at eye level are most likely to be noticed. If vandalism is a major problem, it might be necessary to set the poster-board high up out of reach, but this should only be considered if it will be clearly visible and if a reasonably simple method can be devised for changing the posters.

Construction

The most common shape for a poster-board is a simple rectangle, fixed to a wall, railings or posts. A variation which offers good visibility for people passing in either direction, is two rectangles fixed together in a V-shape. If you are considering installing this type of board, remember that to keep it looking interesting, you will need two posters each time, instead of one.

Two rectangles in a V-shape.

A third possibility is a movable board, which can be placed near the church door or gate, to draw attention to special events. It should be heavy enough not to blow over but light enough to be easily moved about. These boards are not usually glazed (as that would make them rather cumbersome), which means the poster needs to be waterproof.

If a glazed display case is being made locally rather than bought ready made, it is important to specify depth as well as height and width. If the pinboard is set too far back from the glass, the

A movable board.

passer-by will need to stand directly in front of the board to get a clear view of the whole poster. Too wide a frame will increase the problem, obscuring even more of the poster. (If you have inherited a board like this, try inserting an extra layer of pinboard, to bring the poster nearer to the glass).

On the other hand, it is good to have a little space between the glass and the poster (perhaps 10-15mm), so that condensation on the glass does not make paint run, and to allow room for three-dimensional collage, such as crêpe paper flowers or shapes cut out of polystyrene.

Opening method

There are three standard opening methods for display cases:

1 **Hinge.** The most common system is to have the front (glazed) section hinged to the back (pinboard) section so that the front opens like a door. Front opening is more convenient than back opening because you can see what the poster is going to look like while you are putting it up.

2 **Lift-off.** For a small board, the outer (glazed) section can be made to fit over the inner (pinboard) section and lifted right off when the poster needs to be changed.

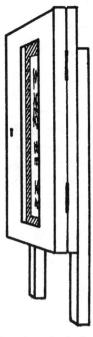

Pinboard too far back and frame too wide.

3 **Sliding.** This method is suitable for a large display-board. The sheet of Perspex is not fixed, but slides to left or right in a groove in the upper and lower sections of the frame. The two side sections of the frame are hinged so that they can be folded back out of the way while the Perspex is moved to one side. When the poster has been changed, the Perspex is pushed back to its central position, and the side sections pulled forward and fixed in place.

Is it necessary to lock the display case? Bear in mind that keys tend to get lost or to be in the wrong place when needed, especially if several people share the job of putting up posters. The ideal system is one that is simple to operate yet not too obvious to would-be vandals. Convenience is the main factor. Even an enthusiast will become discouraged by a weekly battle with a stiff key or awkward screws (especially when fingers are cold!) In reality vandals are

Lift-off frame.

Sliding Perspex.

more likely simply to smash the Perspex (or glass) than to put much effort into working out how to open the display case.

Weatherproofing

Whatever the construction of the glazed board, it must be waterproof when shut. Simply screwing a sheet of Perspex to the front of an existing board will not give sufficient protection for hand-made posters. Glazed boards need some sort of close-fitting frame with a protective 'roof' over the top. Hinges, screws and locks must be of non-rusting metal (aluminium, brass or stainless steel).

Even a waterproof board can be subject to condensation in damp conditions. Ventilation holes in the bottom will help, or try using silica gel moisture absorbers (such as you find included when you buy a pair of sports shoes).

Wind is the other potential hazard. Display cases are vulnerable when open – hinges must be strong enough and sliding Perspex thick enough to withstand a sudden gust of wind while both your hands are fully occupied trying to prevent the poster blowing away!

Glass or acrylic sheet

Assuming the frame and hinges are strong enough to take the weight, ordinary glass is the cheapest option. However, the risk of it being smashed by accident or by vandals probably outweighs the advantage of price. Safety glass is better – it cracks rather than shattering on impact.

Clear polystyrene is cheap but discolours quickly out of doors, needing frequent replacement. Polycarbonate is ideal, but may be beyond the church budget. Acrylic sheet (eg Perspex) is probably the best option. It is lightweight, flexible and tough, although it does scratch rather easily. Light scratches can be removed with metal polish (not glass cleaner or abrasives). For a large board, you need acrylic sheet at least 5mm thick.

Pinboard

Posters can be pasted up, but if they are being changed regularly, and particularly if you want to re-use them later, pins are more convenient. The inside back wall of the display case should be soft enough for comfortable pushing in and removal of drawing pins, yet firm enough to hold them in place.

Wood is too hard. Insulation board (fibreboard) is cheap, soft, lightweight and readily available, but pins can work loose, especially when holes are repeatedly made in the same place. Thick corrugated cardboard can be used as a temporary expedient. (It is also useful as a light, portable display board for workshops).

Cork is very suitable, provided it is thick enough to push the pins right in.

Sundeala is ideal. It is a medium density fibreboard specially designed for notice-boards. It comes in four qualities and various colours, and can be repainted when required. Being made from pulped newspaper, it is also environment-friendly.

Addresses of suppliers can be found on page 152.

Colour

The board should be visible against its surroundings without jarring unpleasantly, especially if the church is an old one. Modern churches are not always easily distinguishable as churches – an eye-catching poster-board can help. The colour of the pinboard can be changed from time to time, using emulsion paint or by covering with paper or fabric. A matt surface looks better than a shiny one.

Give some thought to what colour will be most suitable. A bright orange, for instance, will limit the number of other colours you can use with it, and will tend to draw attention to the board rather than the poster. The best colours are strong but not too bright – royal blue, dark green or a rich, deep red would be suitable. Or you might echo the colour of the church door or railings.

With adequate lighting, posters can proclaim their message twenty-four hours a day, but bear in mind that some street lights alter the look of the colours. If there is no street lighting near your church, you may consider installing special lighting for the poster-board. A soft light is more flattering than one which accentuates every crease and wrinkle.

Vandalism

No system that allows easy access for poster changing will be totally vandal-proof. Prayer is probably the best protection.

Try to judge what sort of reaction your posters are likely to receive. Use humour and aim to arouse curiosity, establishing a rapport with the people walking past rather than provoking antagonism. Avoid texts that seem to condemn (like *'The wages of sin is death'!*)

Thick Perspex is hard to smash, but if you find your board temporarily exposed to the elements, find ways of adapting. Use printed posters, or photocopy simple black and white ones (adding colour with oil pastels or waterproof paint). An unprotected poster casually attached with a couple of drawing pins is an open invitation to vandals (like a loose bit of wallpaper asking to be ripped off). Fix posters firmly with paste or plenty of staples.

EMPTY AND OVERCROWDED NOTICE-BOARDS

There are two extremes to avoid. The empty notice-board gives the impression that nothing is happening, or that those 'in the know' are content to keep their information to themselves. The overcrowded board looks busy but confusing.

The empty board

If you cannot make enough posters to keep up a constant supply:

1 **Printed posters** (bought or borrowed) can be used to supplement the hand-made ones.

2 **Be aware of events** in your own church or other churches that you can help to publicise.

3 **Change the posters regularly,** even if you only have a few to choose from, finding a variety of ways of displaying them.

4 **Encourage other people** to take a turn at making and putting up posters. It is hard to remain enthusiastic if you work alone.

The overcrowded board

Usually seen inside the church rather than outside, the overcrowded board is almost as unhelpful as the empty one. A jumble of small notices, where none stand out clearly against the others, becomes part of the wallpaper, a neutral background that does not attract any interest.

Installing extra notice-boards, each with a specific function, would be one solution. The other is to find more effective ways of using what you have.

Most people, most of the time, do not notice notices. If you don't think this is true, try asking a few people in your church what is on the notice-board this week. Even though they may have intended to, they probably forgot, or did not have time, or did not know where to look. We need to find ways of making notices noticeable.

A general church notice-board is likely to have two functions: providing regular information and drawing attention to unusual events. It is important to plan what is on the board so that people can find what they want quickly and easily.

Regular notices, such as the flower or cleaning rota, do not need to be particularly eye-catching. They should be put up in the same place and presented in the same format each time so that the people concerned know where to look and what to look for.

Occasional information, by contrast, needs to stand out clearly to have any effect. This can be achieved in various ways. See page 93 *(Planning)* for ways of attracting attention.

If the Sunday School, the Keep Fit group, the flower rota, missionary news, prayer requests and holiday postcards all share one board, it is wise to appoint a notice-board coordinator. A little skilful rearrangement can draw attention to whatever is most important at any particular time.

If the job falls to you, a word of caution: make sure that, if drama happens to be your main interest, it is not always the drama group poster that takes centre stage.

Hints for effective use of a shared notice board

1 **Eliminate anything out-of-date.**

2 **Group notices together** according to subject, under clear headings such as 'Missionary', 'Prayer', 'Housegroups'.

3 **Notices can overlap** slightly, especially if similar subjects are linked, but do not obscure important information.

4 **Coloured backing paper** can draw attention to one item, or link together a group of related notices.

5 **Reorganise** the board from time to time and find fresh ways of presenting information to stimulate interest.

6 **Spotlight one area** of church life at a time rather than giving equal weight to everything.

7 **Create space** around the item you want to emphasise by moving others closer together.

8 **The best position is at eye-level** and towards the centre of the notice board. Information aimed at children should be lower than for adults.

9 **Large posters will overpower** the standard-size notices and might be better elsewhere.

10 **Be sensitive** to the requirements of other church members and ask for their comments.

Remember that if the notice-board is regularly changed and always looks interesting and attractive, people are more likely to form the habit of looking at it.

Group notices together.

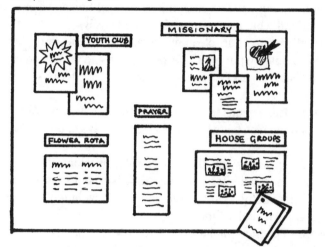

Coloured backing paper.

Create space.

USING SMALL PRINTED PUBLICITY POSTERS

Posters printed for church events are often only A4 size, which is fine for indoor notice-boards, or to stick in a shop window, but too small to create much impact on a large board outside the church. On the plus side, you will probably find plenty of spares to cut up and experiment with, because it is cheaper (per copy) to print large numbers.

Some ideas for making small posters more eye-catching

1 **Several copies** of the same poster can be used, slightly overlapping, on one board

   - in a straight or curved line,

   - in a shape that echoes the design of the poster,

   - in the shape of a letter (eg the first letter of the title of the event).

   Try to arrange them so that the most important information is visible on each poster.

2 **Add photocopies.** If you only have one printed poster, arrange photocopies behind it to look like a repeated shadow.

3 **Make some posters bulge.** Add interest by squeezing the sides slightly together before you push in the pins, so that the middle bulges out.

4 **Roll the poster loosely** so that a selected portion of information or picture is clearly visible, and attach in front of, or alongside, flat copies of the same poster.

5 **Coloured backing sheets** used with imagination will improve the display. (See pages 132-133.)

6 **Cut and spread.** Cut the small poster into its component parts and arrange them on a larger sheet of paper. Don't be afraid of the extra space. Make an interesting design by grouping elements together, rather than dotting them evenly on the paper. If the title is isolated in an area of empty space, it will stand out.

7 **Enlarge** all or part of the poster to a size suitable for your display area. This is the best solution, if you have time. As far as possible, use the same colours and lettering style as the original, so that it is immediately obvious that your poster is advertising the same event as small ones seen elsewhere.

   Cut large letters out of coloured card or, if the lettering is black, enlarge it on the photocopier. If you are short of time, cut out a single huge initial letter to attract attention. It is not necessary to enlarge all the secondary information, provided the main title and picture are bold and clear – less important sections can be cut straight from the original poster and arranged on the new backing. Leave out anything non-essential.

USING SMALL PRINTED POSTERS

Several copies in a curved line.

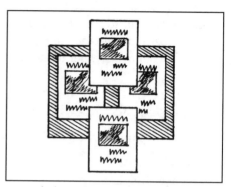

A shape that echoes the design.

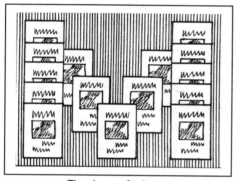

The shape of a letter.

Photocopies like a repeated shadow.

Make the posters bulge out . . .

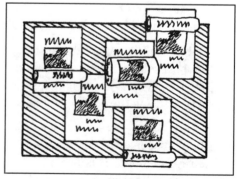

or roll them.

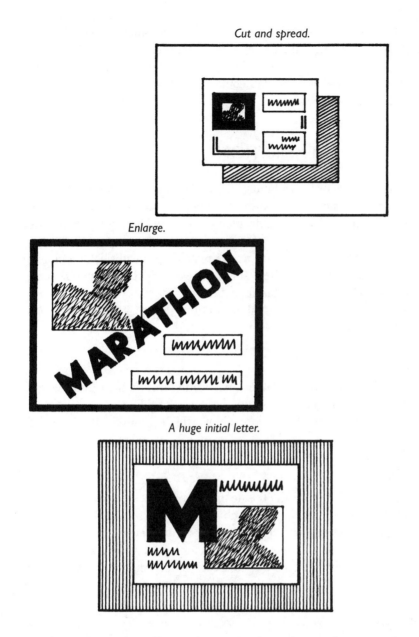

Cut and spread.

Enlarge.

A huge initial letter.

8 **Découpage** – literally 'cutting out' – is an interesting way of creating a three-dimensional effect. Cut out the picture (or main title) from one copy of the poster and stick it on top of the same element on a second poster, with something behind the cut-out to raise it a little. Blobs of silicone glue or pieces of foam board are ideal (if you can find them in a craft shop). Otherwise use bath sealant or corrugated cardboard.

Using several copies of the same poster, you can create a multi-layered picture. Leave one poster intact, and cut out selected design elements from the others. Stick the first cut-out on the uncut poster, using silicone glue, sealant, foam or cardboard to raise it. Successive cut-outs will each be smaller than the one before. For example, if using a picture of a vase of flowers, you would cut both vase and flowers the first time, the second time just the flowers, and for the third you would select just a few flowers. You could then, if you wish, curl the petals slightly and add a coat of varnish.

EXHIBITIONS

Don't be frightened by the word 'exhibition'. It simply means 'showing', which is, after all, what posters are made for. It can be as simple as half a dozen Christmas posters made by the Sunday School children and put up in the church porch for everyone to see.

Once you have an enthusiastic group of poster-makers, you will start to build up a stock of posters. Rather than leaving them stored away where they cannot be seen, consider holding an exhibition, to stimulate further interest within your own church, to introduce the idea of poster-making to other local Christians and as a means of outreach to non-churchgoers.

Start small

Start with an informal mini-exhibition, rather than waiting till you have hundreds of posters. If you wait too long, you will either have the problem of organising a massive exhibition or face difficult decisions about which posters to include and which to leave out.

Themed exhibitions

If you have organised a workshop on the theme of Harvest, or a series on the Lord's Prayer, put the resulting posters up in the church straight away so that everyone can see them. You might collect together Easter posters from several churches and display them at a central venue. Or choose posters that have pictures of flowers, and see if other people in the church would like to create arrangements of real flowers to complement them.

Larger exhibitions

While it is easier to plan frequent informal displays, it is worth having a larger exhibition from time to time, making it a special occasion rather than just another day in the life of the church. Try to involve as many church members as possible in different ways – setting up display boards, arranging flowers, serving coffee, inviting friends and welcoming visitors – so that they feel it is their event as well as yours. People who do not normally come to church will sometimes come in out of curiosity if they think something unusual is going on.

A well-organised exhibition is worth publicising. Design an attractive mini-poster which can be photocopied and sent out to other churches and displayed in local

PIN OR STICK?

PINNING

Drawing pins	Use a colour that blends with the poster. You want the poster to be noticed, not the pins.
Map pins	These have a small coloured head and are neat and unobtrusive.
Sewing pins	Cheap, readily available and almost invisible, they are a useful standby, provided the pinboard is soft enough.
Staples	No need to buy a staple gun – an ordinary paper stapler works well on pinboard, and the staples will be easy to remove afterwards. Simply open it out and press firmly. The staples go straight into the board rather than folding flat as they do on paper.

STICKING

Paste	Wallpaper paste can be used out of doors if you have an unprotected wooden board, but it may be difficult to remove the poster intact.
Blu-tack	Looking like a lump of well-chewed chewing gum, Blu-tack is useful for temporary sticking of light posters on gloss-painted or varnished wood, glass or sound emulsioned walls. It can be used over and over again.
Masking tape	A loop of masking tape (sticky side out), used like Blutack, is flat and neat under thin paper.
Double-sided tape	This is convenient to use but hard to remove from the poster, so take care when storing posters afterwards.
Sticky fixers	These small squares of plastic foam are sticky on both sides, for permanent fixing on smooth hard surfaces.
Velcro tabs	Hundreds of tiny nylon hooks give a firm hold on fabric- or felt-covered boards, but also allow easy repositioning. For economy they can be cut in two or four (they are very strong, especially on loop nylon fabric).

shops. Send details to your local newspaper, radio or TV station a week or so in advance. If the event sounds interesting, they might decide to cover it as a feature or news item. In any case, find out whether they provide a free 'What's On' service. During the exhibition, the best way of catching the eye of passers-by is to hang a colourful banner over the church door.

The success or failure of any exhibition, however small, depends as much on how the posters are displayed as on the posters themselves, so it is worth spending time praying and planning. Be particularly careful about any posters displayed at the front of church, where they will be a focus of attention during worship. Humorous ones may be better near the entrance, to relax first-time visitors.

CREATIVITY AND ORDER

One year, while setting up a poster exhibition in our church, I had a crisis of confidence. I knew it was important to do the job as well as possible, but was I fussing too much about details? Did it really matter how many centimetres we allowed between this poster and the next, or what colour backing we used? Perhaps a haphazard arrangement would be just as effective. I asked the Lord for guidance and when I looked at my Bible notes for that day, the reading was *Proverbs 8*. In verses *27-31* the voice of Wisdom says:

> *'I was there when he set the heavens in place,*
>   *when he marked out the horizon...*
> *when he established the clouds above*
>   *and fixed securely the fountains of the deep,*
> *when he gave the sea its boundary...*
> *and when he marked out the foundations of the earth.*
>   *Then I was the craftsman at his side.*
> *I was filled with delight day after day,*
>   *rejoicing always in his presence,*
> *rejoicing in his whole world*
>   *and delighting in mankind.'*

I was reassured by the feeling that God was, and is, concerned about the practical details as well as the overall concept. I like the verbs *'set in place'*, *'marked out'*, *'established'*, *'fixed securely'*, *'gave its boundary'*. The creative process can be precise in its planning and execution, as well as being dynamic and varied.

God has given us many different talents and we need not be afraid to use them. If we have eyes open to the beauty of God's Creation, ears alert for his instructions and hands ready to do his work, we too will be *'filled with delight... rejoicing in his presence... and delighting in mankind'*.

Posters to buy

The following firms supply posters by mail order. Phone or write for a catalogue.

POSTERS SUITABLE FOR OUTSIDE THE CHURCH

CPO (Christian Publicity Organisation)
Garcia Estate, Canterbury Road, Worthing, West Sussex BN13 1BW (Tel 01903-264556).
A regularly updated range of well-designed, full-colour posters to suit all tastes. Some co-ordinate with other publicity items such as invitation cards, folders, tracts, stickers, balloons and even T-shirts. Four types of poster (available in a variety of sizes):
- Blank posters (designs to which you can add your own information)
- Message posters (attractive pictures with a biblical message)
- Slogan Posters (snappy catch-phrases)
- Eyecatcher posters (designed to make people think).

SGM International
Radstock House, 3 Eccleston Street, London SW1W 9LZ (Tel 0171-730 2155).
Large, glossy posters, each with a clear Bible text superimposed on a colour photo.

St Paul Multimedia Productions
Middle Green, Langley, Slough, Berks SL3 6BS (Tel 01753-577629).
Some striking and unusual posters, especially the Turvey Abbey ones, which are laminated for extra protection.

Gospel Posters
8 Manstone Lane, Sidmouth, Devon EX10 9TS (Tel 01395-577507).
Bold screen-printed designs with a message that can be read at a glance.

Decade Ministries
Grove House, Limetrees, Chilton, Oxon OX11 OHY (Tel 01235-833030).
Slogans printed in black letters on Day-glo paper, laminated or plastic encapsulated if you wish. Also available: a large range of amusing visuals you can use to design your own posters.

Victory Posters
Portland Road, London SE25 4PN (Tel 0181-656 2297).
Large, illustrated Bible texts.

Bible Text Publicity Mission
PO Box 2704, Billericay, Essex CM12 9BL (Tel 01277-626309).
Scripture posters (two-colour, with picture), used in railway stations, but also offered for sale to churches.

Trinitarian Bible Society
Tyndale House, Dorset Road, London SW19 3NN (Tel 0181-543 7857).
Two-colour Scripture text (words only). Authorized Version.

Fellowship for Evangelising Britain's Villages
PO Box 271, Taunton, Somerset TA1 1YY (Tel 01823-321016).
Bible texts, four sizes (words only, black on white). Could be made more attractive by mounting on a sheet of wrapping paper to add a colourful border.

Religious Society of Friends (Quakers)
Friends Book Centre, Friends House, 173-177 Euston Road, London NW1 2BJ (Tel 0171-387 3601).
A variety of posters on subjects such as peace, social responsibility and education.

SMALLER POSTERS SUITABLE FOR INDOOR USE

Spearhead
Unit 7, Huffwood Trading Estate, Brookers Road, Billingshurst, West Sussex RH14 9UR (Tel 01403-785785).
Extensive range of beautiful colour photographs with superimposed Bible verses. Some posters large enough to use outside, but the words are more easily read at close range.

Argus Posters
Antioch Ltd, Unit 9, Pipers Lane Estate, Thatcham, Berks RG19 4NA (Tel 01635-294700).
A varied range of styles including photos, calligraphy and humour.

Palm Tree Posters
Kevin Mayhew Ltd, Maypole Farm, Buxhall, Stowmarket, Suffolk IP14 3DJ (Tel 01449-737978).
Colour photos with biblical quotations and meditations.

The Joseph Flow
49 Cromer Road, Norwich, Norfolk NR6 6LX (Tel 01603-406591).
Colourful, detailed Bible-story pictures for children to explore and enjoy.

Bible Lands Trading
PO Box 50, High Wycombe, Buckinghamshire, HP15 7QU (Tel 01494-521351).
Posters to match their colourful folders.

POSTERS MADE TO YOUR SPECIFICATIONS

Computer-generated

Christian Editions
17 Golden Plover Close, Custom House, Victoria Docks, London E16 3EG (Tel 0171-366 9559).

Hand-painted

Cyril E Smith
Gospel Posters, 8 Manstone Lane, Sidmouth, EX10 9 TS (Tel 01395-577507)

MISSION AND AID AGENCIES

Several missionary societies regularly bring out new and imaginative posters. Some posters, with Bible texts, are suitable for general use; others illustrate aspects of the specific work of each organisation. Here are a few to try:

Tear Fund
100 Church Road, Teddington, Middlesex TW11 8QE (Tel 0181-977 9144).

Christian Aid
PO Box 100, London SE1 7RT (Tel 0171-620 4444).

CAFOD
Romero Close, Stockwell Road, London SW9 9TY (Tel 0171-733 7900).

Mid-Africa Ministry (CMS)
157 Waterloo Road, London SE1 8UU (Tel 0171-261 1370).

Interserve
325 Kennington Road, London SE11 4QH (Tel 0171-735 8227).

Bible Society
Stonehill Green, Westlea, Swindon, Wiltshire SN5 7DG (Tel 01793-418100).

Display equipment

EXTERIOR POSTER-BOARDS

The following firms sell a variety of poster-boards for outdoor use. To help you make an informed decision about the best type for your church, check pages 134-139 (*Display*).

Silvercases
Woodcon Products Ltd, Daux Road, Billingshurst, West Sussex RH14 9SR (Tel 01403-784671).

Arien
99 Church Street, Highbridge, Somerset TA9 3HR (Tel 01278-785268 or 780331).

Greenbarnes Displays
Unit K1, Lincoln Court, Borough Road, Buckingham Road Industrial Estate, Brackley, Northants NN13 7BE (Tel 01280-701093).

Wilson and Garden Ltd
Newtown Street, Kilsyth, Glasgow G65 0JX (Tel 01236-823291).

Ambassador Enterprises
Portland Road, London SE25 4PN (Tel 0181-656 2297).

John Derrick
Westby, Sharpham Road, Cheddar, Somerset BS27 3DR (Tel 01934-742522).

INTERIOR DISPLAY-BOARDS

Many different display systems are available for indoor use, both wall-mounted and free-standing. If you are buying a set of free-standing boards, check the following points first:

- Are they light and easy to carry?
- Are they suitable for both pins and Velcro tabs?
- Are they easy to set up and dismantle?
- Can they be joined together in various ways to make interesting displays, but also used separately?
- Are they big enough to accommodate posters in different arrangements?
- If not in permanent use, are they convenient to store and can they be transported in an average car?
- Are they at eye level? Unless needed as screens, or for small children, boards that go right down to the floor are of relatively little use.

Suppliers

SD Systems Ltd
Lancaster Road, Cressex Business Park, High Wycombe, Bucks HP12 3PY (Tel 01494-465212).

Axis Visual Presentation
Covloc House, Quinn Close, Seven Stars Estate, Whitley, Coventry, West Midlands CV3 4LH (Tel 01203-639772).

Pergola Products Ltd
Leigh Court, Leigh Street, High Wycombe, Bucks HP11 2QU (Tel 01494-520495).

Nobo (UK) Ltd
Alder Close, Eastbourne, Sussex BN23 6QB (Tel 01323-641521).

Unique Visual Communication Equipment
Wilson and Garden Ltd (see address above).

Librex Educational Ltd
Colwick Road, Nottingham NG2 4BG
(Tel 0115-950 4664 or 1115-958 0032).

Sundeala
Warwick House, 27/31 St Mary's Road,
Ealing, London W5 5PR (Tel 0181-579 0811).
    Wall-mounted notice-boards only.

PINBOARD SUPPLIERS

Sundeala
(address above)
    Medium density fibreboard in a variety
    of qualities and colours.

Siesta Cork Tiles Ltd
Unit 21, Tait Road, Gloucester Road,
Croydon, Surrey CR0 2DP
(Tel 0181-683 4055).
    Composition cork in rolls, as well as
    various natural and dark coloured cork
    tiles.

C Olley & Sons Ltd
Iberia House, Finchley Avenue, Mildenhall,
Suffolk IP28 7BJ (Tel 01638-712076).
    Cork to suit individual requirements.
    Phone for details.

Materials by mail order

Some suppliers stipulate a minimum order or charge quite heavily for postage and packing, so find out first whether there is a local educational supplier you can use. If not, could you share an order with your church's Sunday School or Mums and Toddlers Group, or with a local school?

GENERAL ART MATERIALS

London Graphic Centre
16-18 Shelton Street, Covent Garden, London WC2H 9JJ (Tel 0171-240 0095).
   Almost everything the poster-maker might need.

Daler-Rowney
12 Percy Street, Tottenham Court Road, London W1A 2BP (Tel 0171-636 8241).
   Fine art materials.

N E S Arnold Ltd
Ludlow Hill Road, West Bridgford, Nottingham NG2 6HD (Tel 0115-945 2200).

Galt Educational
Culveot Street, Oldham, Lancs OL4 2ST (Tel 0161-627 5086).

Hope Education Ltd
Orb Mill, Huddersfield Road, Oldham, Lancs OL4 2ST (Tel 0161-633 6611).

Asco Educational Supplies Ltd
19 Lockwood Way, Parkside Lane, Leeds LS11 5TH (Tel 0113-270 7070).

County Supplies and Services Ltd
County House, Commercial Road, Reading, Berks RG2 0RB (Tel 01734-755774).

Step by Step Ltd
Lavenham Road, Beeches Trading Estate, Yate, Bristol BS17 5QX (Tel 01454-320200).

Early Learning Centre
Mail Order Department, South Marston Park, Swindon SN3 4TJ (Tel 01793-832832).
   Simple art materials for pre-school children.

LARGE-SIZE CALLIGRAPHY PENS

See page 84 *(Lettering)* and page 114 *(Materials)*.

Blot's Pen & Ink Supplies
Units 67-68, Bury Business Centre, Kay Street, Bury, Lancs BL9 6BU (Tel 0161-705 1878).

Manuscript Pen Company Ltd
Highley, Near Brignorth, Shropshire WV16 6NN (Tel 01746-861236).

Philip Poole & Co Ltd
105 Great Russell Street, London WC1B 3RY (Tel 0171-636 1045).

Falkiner Fine Papers Ltd
76 Southampton Row, London WC1B 4AR (Tel 0171-831 1151).

London Graphic Centre
(address above).

Relevant books

POSTER-MAKING

The Art of Poster Making by John Smith (published by Osmiroid in 1989, ISBN 1-871517-20-6). Price £4.95.
> A slim book, informative and easy to read.

*Design and Print your own Posters by J I Biegeleisen (Watson-Guptill, New York, 1984, ISBN 0-8230-1310-3).
> Out of print, but full of useful information if you can find a copy.

The One Minute Poster by Patricia R Dunmire (Gospel Light, 1991, ISBN 0-8307-1442-1).
> Posters to photocopy – add your own information.

DIY Posters and Banners by Paul Wade (Printforce Ltd, 50 York Road, Cheam, Surrey SM2 6HH, ISBN 0-948834-81-1). Price £2.75.
> Large letters and clip art to photocopy.

Very few books specifically about poster-making have been published in recent years, but some from the 1960's and 70's can still be found in libraries, or picked up cheaply second-hand.

HISTORY OF POSTERS

The Power of the Poster by Margaret Timmers (V & A Publications, 1998, ISBN 1-85177-2405).
> Published to coincide with the exhibition of the same name held at the Victoria & Albert Museum in London.

Posters American Style by Therese Thau Heyman (Harry N Abrams Inc, New York, 1998, ISBN 0-8109-3749-2).
> To coincide with the exhibition at the Smithsonian Institution, Washington DC.

Posters: a Concise History by John Barnicoat (Thames and Hudson, World of Art series, ISBN 0-500-20118-8). Price £6.95.

*The Poster: a Worldwide Survey and History by Alain Weill (English edition by Sotheby's Publications, 1985, ISBN 0-85667-309-9).

The Modern Poster by Stuart Wrede (The Museum of Modern Art, New York, 1988, ISBN 0-87070-571-7).

SPECIFIC CATEGORIES OF POSTERS

Underground Art: London Transport Posters 1908 to the Present by Oliver Green (Laurence King, 1999, ISBN 1-85669-166-7).

By Underground to Kew:London Transport Posters 1908 to the Present by Jonathan Riddell and William T Stearn (Studio Vista, 1994, ISBN 0-289-80141-9).

By Underground to the Zoo: London Transport Posters 1913 to the Present by Jonathan Riddell and Peter Denton (Studio Vista, 1995, ISBN 0-289-80133-8).

Railway Posters 1923-1947 by Beverley Cole and Richard Durack (Laurence King, 1992, ISBN 1-85669-014-8).

Happy Holidays: the Golden Age of Railway Posters by Michael Palin (Pavilion, 1998, ISBN 1-86205-189-5).

*Toulouse-Lautrec: the Complete Posters by Russell Ash (Pavilion Books, 1991, ISBN 1-85145-517-5).

The Complete 'Masters of the Poster' by Stanley Appelbaum (Dover Publications, ISBN 0-486-26309-6).

The Posters of Jules Chéret by Lucy Broido (Dover Publications, ISBN 0-486-26966-3).

*Twentieth Century Posters: Chagall, Braque, Picasso, Dufy, Matisse, Miró, Léger by Fernand Mourlot (Wellfleet Press, 1989, ISBN 1-55521-385-5).

DESIGN

The Non-Designer's Design Book by Robin Williams (Peachpit Press, Berkeley, California, 1994, ISBN 1-56609-159-4). Price £15.99.
> Basic design principles, applicable to hand-made as well as computer-generated posters. Everyone involved in church publicity should read this book! Available from Sunrise Software (see page 157).

A Smile in the Mind: witty thinking in graphic design by Beryl Mc Alhone and David Stuart (Phaidon Press, 1998, ISBN 0-7148-3812-8) Price £22.95.
> A wonderful book, full of deceptively simple ideas that will keep you smiling from cover to cover.

*Graphic Idea Notebook by Jan V White (Pitman Publishing, 1980, ISBN 0-8230-2149-1).
> Brilliantly stimulating source book, sadly out of print.

CALLIGRAPHY

Colour Calligraphy by Barbara Bundy (Osmiroid, 1989, ISBN 1-871517-05-2). Price £4.95.
Colour Calligraphy by David Graham (Search Press, 1991, ISBN 0-85532-609-3). Price £4.95.

*Layout and Design for Calligraphers by Alan Furber (Dryad Press, 1985, ISBN 0-8521-9617-2).
> Clear examples demonstrate the principles of good layout. Highly recommended.

The Little Manual of Calligraphy by Charles Pearce (Harper Collins, 1992, ISBN 0-00-411811-1). Price £3.99.

CLIP ART

See separate list (page 157).

CUT PAPER TECHNIQUES

Fun with Paper Sculpture by Clive Stevens (Search Press, 1998, ISBN 0-85532-862-2). Price £5.95.

The Art and Craft of Paper Sculpture by Paul Jackson (Apple Press, 1996, ISBN 1-85076-725-4). Price £12.99.

Three-Dimensional Découpage by Vivien Crook (Search Press, 1996, ISBN 0-85532-808-8), price £5.95.

Creative Three-Dimensional Découpage by Debbie Sellers (Search Press, 1998, ISBN 0-85532-863-3), price £8.95.

The Art and Craft of Paper by Faith Shannon (Mitchell Beazley, 1996, ISBN 1-85732-964-3). Price £16.99.

DISPLAY

Display by Rhona Whiteford and Jim Fitzsimmonds (Scholastic Publications, 1988, ISBN 0-590-70950-X).
Creative Display by Lynne Burgess (Scholastic Publications, 1991, ISBN 0-590-76506-X).
> Aimed at primary school teachers, these books are a useful source of display ideas.

CHURCH BANNER-MAKING

Making and Using Banners, for Witness, Proclamation and Celebration by Priscilla Nunnerley and Ruth Wood (Gazelle Books, 1998, ISBN 1-899746-08-0). Price £8.99.

Banners around the World by Priscilla Nunnerley with Ruth Wood. (Christian Banners with Nuprint/Gazelle Books, 1994, ISBN 0-9509307-3-3). Price £6.95.

Banner books from Concordia Publishing House, 3558 South Jefferson Avenue, Saint Louis MO, 63118-3968, USA:
> **Banners for Worship** by Carol Jean Harms (ISBN 0-570-04492-8)

Banner Patterns for Worship by
Carol Jean Harms (0-570-04491-X).
Quick and Easy Banner Designs by
Carol Jean Harms (0-570-04842-7).
Banners with a Conscience by Dale A
Bargmann (0-570-04897-4).
His Banner over me is Love by Dale
A Bargmann (0-570-04818-4).
Raise a Banner to the Lord by Dale A
Bargmann (0-570-04626-2).
Banners on Favorite Bible Verses by
Sally Beck (0-570-04988-1).

**Raising Standards: a Handbook for
Banner Makers** by Anne McAlpine,
Maggie Lunan and Naomi Lidwell.
Obtainable from Renfield St Stephens
Church Centre, 260 Bath Street, Glasgow
G2 4JP. Price £5.00, including p&p.

*The Banner Book by Betty Wolfe
(published by Morehouse-Barlowe in the
United States).
> Out of print, but very good if you can
> find a copy.

**How to design and make banners for
sacred and secular festivals** by Angela
Dewar and Gisela Banbury (Search Press,
ISBN 0-85532-681-6). Price £5.95.

CHRISTIAN ART AND CREATIVITY

**Art and Music Toolkit: Creative ideas
for using the Bible in the classroom** by
Margaret Cooling (Bible Society, 1996,
ISBN 0-564-08855-2). Price £13.99.

**What a Good Idea! Activities for
children in the church** (National
Christian Education Council, 1992,
ISBN 0-7197-0784-6). Price £8.45.

**Picture It! How God can use your
artistic gifts** by Paul Clowney (Bible
Society, 1987, ISBN 0-564-07792-5).

Let your Artist out! by William Denning
(Hunt & Thorpe, 1992, ISBN 1-85608-185-0).
Available from the author at
Maypole Farm, Lower Morton, Thornbury,
Bristol BS12 1LE. Price £2.99.

The Creative Heart of God by Ruth
Goring (Harold Shaw, Wheaton, Illinois,
1997, ISBN 0-87788-145-6).
> Group Bible studies about Christian
> creativity.

Doorposts by Timothy Botts (Bible
Society, ISBN 0-564-04383-4). Price £12.50.
> An inspiring collection of calligraphic
> renderings of Bible verses.

CHURCH PUBLICITY

How to Promote your Church by Anne
Coomes and Andy Radford (Church House
Publishing, 1995, ISBN 0-7151-4865-6).
Price £3.00.

**Keep in touch! A practical guide to help
churches improve their
communications** by Peter Crumpler
(Scripture Union, 1993, ISBN 0-86201-814-5).
Price £5.95.

**Making Contact: Christian
communication and the local church** by
Rob Marshall (Bible Society, 1993,
ISBN 0-564-08445-X). Price £5.95.

***Message on a Shoestring: a publicity
handbook** by Chris Radley (Marc Europe,
1986, ISBN 0-947697-37-3).

Let's Get Publicity by David Saint
(Printforce – see address on page 154.
ISBN 0-948834-221-8). Price £4.50.

* Asterisk means book is out of print.

Clip art sources

CHRISTIAN CLIP ART ON COMPUTER DISC OR CD:
(Send for a catalogue)

Sunrise Software
PO Box 19, Carlisle, CA3 0BR
(Tel 0845-0579579)

Christian Computer Art
33 Bramley Way, Hardwick,
Cambridge CB3 7XD (Tel 01954-210009)

Churchill Systems
PO Box 32, Tadcaster,
North Yorks LS24 9YA (Tel 01937-530200).

McCrimmons
Freepost, CL2425, Southend-on-Sea,
Essex SS3 0BR.

Evangelsoft Ltd
PO Box 224, Kingston upon Thames,
Surrey KT1 2NX (Tel 0181-549 2280).

Exousia Christian Software
53 Hindes Road, Harrow HA1 1SQ
(Tel 0181-424 0900).

KAB Services
2 Wynlea Close, Crawley Down, West
Sussex RH10 4HP (Tel 01342-716370).
Canon Starwriter specialist.

CLIP ART MAINLY IN BOOK OR SHEET FORM:

Palm Tree Press
Kevin Mayhew Ltd, Rattlesden, Bury St
Edmunds, Suffolk IP30 0SZ
(Tel 01449-737978).
Clip art books geared to church needs.
The most useful for posters is Instant
Art for Publicity.

Gospel Light
Ventura, CA 93006, USA
Church Ministry Clip Art Book and
Church Bulletin Clip Art Book. Also clip
art on disc.

The Church Union
Faith House, 7 Tufton Street,
London SW1P 3QN (0171-222 6952).
Various books and discs, eg Clip Art for
the Liturgical Year.

Christian Publicity Organisation
Garcia Estate, Canterbury Road, Worthing,
West Sussex BN13 1BW (Tel 01903-264556).
Graphic symbols, on paper or disc, to
design your own publicity posters.

Church News Service
37b New Cavendish Street,
London W1M 8JR.
Monthly illustrations, cartoons,
headings and frames, intended for
church magazines but can be used for
posters.

Dover Publications
The Dover Bookshop, 18 Earlham Street,
London WC2H 9LN (Tel 0171-836 2111).
Big range of attractive, reasonably-
priced books, covering all aspects of
design, illustration and lettering, widely
available in high street bookshops. Mail
order catalogue available from the
address above.

Lexis International Ltd
PO Box 349, Guernsey GY1 3UZ
(Tel 01481-51975).
Their Artfile series includes People,
Photo Images, Creatures and Sport.

Printforce
(Address on page 154).
DIY Posters and Banners – large letters
and clip art images.

COPYING BY HAND:

CPAS (Church Pastoral Aid Society)
Athena Drive, Tachbrook Park,
Warwick CV34 6NG (Tel 01926-334242).
Help, I can't draw! – simple figures and
scenes to trace or copy by hand if you
don't have a computer or photocopier.

Index